Francesca Romana Rinaldi

FASHION INDUSTRY 2030

Reshaping the Future
Through Sustainability
and Responsible Innovation

Foreword by
Matteo Marzotto

Afterword by
Matteo Ward

Cover: Illustration by Francesca Mariani (www.francescamariani.com)
Typesetting: Laura Panigara, Cesano Boscone (MI)

Copyright © 2019 Bocconi University Press
EGEA S.p.A.

EGEA S.p.A.
Via Salasco, 5 - 20136 Milano
Tel. 02/5836.5751 – Fax 02/5836.5753
egea.edizioni@unibocconi.it – www.egeaeditore.it

All rights reserved, including but not limited to translation, total or partial adaptation, reproduction, and communication to the public by any means on any media (including microfilms, films, photocopies, electronic or digital media), as well as electronic information storage and retrieval systems. For more information or permission to use material from this text, see the website www.egeaeditore.it

Given the characteristics of Internet, the publisher is not responsible for any changes of address and contents of the websites mentioned.

First edition: October 2019

ISBN Domestic Edition	978889990261-2
ISBN International Edition	978888548695-9
ISBN Epub and Mobipocket International Edition	978888548696-6

"Finally, a point of view that is going to change the way we look at the future of the Fashion Industry! Francesca has been able to drive attention to something still hidden to many managers and to capture raising ways to manage our business."
Giorgio Ravasio, Country Manager at Vivienne Westwood Italy

"Francesca takes the high road, and will hopefully lead businesses in the fashion industry to critically look at their operations and adopt more responsible business practices."
Yannick Meijers, Sales Manager Eastern Europe & MEA at Patagonia

"*Fashion Industry 2030* is a concrete book for anyone who wants to know how transparency, traceability, circularity and collaborative consumption are affecting the industry. Education towards new business models is nowadays fundamental to contribute to a better world through responsible fashion."
Sara Sozzani Maino, Deputy Director Special Projects of Vogue Italia, Head of Vogue Talents, International Brand Ambassador Camera Nazionale della Moda Italiana

"*Fashion Industry 2030* explores this radical and permanent shift towards a hopeful and better future. I believe it is worth reading because of its rigorous approach – based on observation, figures, trends, market behaviours, best practices – and its brave assertion that things for the complex fashion pipeline have to change. Now and forever."
Matteo Marzotto, President of Dondup

"This book provides the inspiration and the tools for a new generation of leaders in the fashion industry to take on their role with the understanding that they will have to re-imagine it. Opening up the industry to embrace a necessary shift from the cur-

rent and static situation of linear individualism to a state of circular collectivism, with an inclusive mindset which will see the market, our customers, taking on a more active role – all united in their diversity for a stronger future."
Matteo Ward, Co-founder and CEO of WRÅD

"The Fashion Industry is in constant change and it is hard to foresee its evolution. This book, through a complete and rigorous analysis of the current situation and an informed prediction of what lies ahead, gives managers and leaders an outstanding tool to prepare them for the future of the fashion industry and the value that resides in making conscious choices."
Francesco Cuccarolo, Sustainability Lead at YOOX NET-A-PORTER GROUP

Looking forward to immersing myself in this new book by Francesca Romana Rinaldi, knowing that it will reiterate and strengthen my own beliefs: that in order to achieve a best in practice value chain for the fashion industry we need to think outside boxes, implement rigour as well as creativity, and work together for our future."
Orsola de Castro, Co-founder of Fashion Revolution

"Francesca's book gives a much deeper perspective on how to read the organic evolution of the fashion industry."
Albert Candiani, Owner of Candiani Denim

"Francesca's book gives us an overall and tangible view of how the fashion industry will evolve. What is not sustainable, won't be fashionable anymore."
Pierre-Vincent Dor, LVMH Italy CSR & Sustainability Specialist

*To the women of my heart:
Adelina, Gioia, Rossella and Tea.
Thank you for being my family,
genuine inspiration sources,
strongest supporters,
best friends
and
fun playmates.*

Table of Contents

Foreword by *Matteo Marzotto*	XIII
List of Acronyms	XV
Introduction by *Francesca Romana Rinaldi*	1
Credits	5
Acknowledgements	5

1 The Relevance of Responsible Innovation in Fashion 7
  by *Francesca Romana Rinaldi*
  1.1 Fashion industry and sustainability: synonyms or oxymoron? 7
  1.2 Increasing interest in CSR 9
  1.3 From shareholder to shared value 10
  1.4 The Responsible Fashion Company 13
  1.5 Responsible innovation: the missing ingredient! 14
  References 15

2 One Size Doesn't Fit All 19
  by *Francesca Romana Rinaldi*
  2.1 Defining the consumers interested in sustainability 19
  2.2 Does one size fit all? 23
  2.3 SDG 12 and sustainable communication in fashion 26
  2.4 Millennials vs Gen Z: consumer expectations about sustainable fashion 32
  References 35

3 Crafting Innovative Business Models in Fashion 37
  by *Francesca Romana Rinaldi*
  3.1 Innovative business models in fashion 37

	3.2 The active role of consumers	39
	3.3 Main drivers of change in fashion: traceability and transparency, circularity, collaborative consumption	43
	3.4 Responsible innovation: a Renewed Fashion Value Chain model	49
	3.5 The importance of grassroots innovations for sustainability	53
	References	57
4	**Enhancing Transparency and Traceability for Sustainable Value Chains in the Garment and Footwear Industry** by *Maria Teresa Pisani*	**59**
	4.1 A globalized industry with an enormous environmental footprint and societal risks	60
	4.2 Transparency and traceability as a means to enhance sustainability of a complex and opaque value chain	61
	4.3 Companies' strategies for sustainable production patterns	64
	4.4 Meeting an ever-increasing demand for trusted information	66
	4.5 Challenges and opportunities to achieving value chain traceability and transparency	69
	4.6 Policy and legislation in support of transparency and traceability of value chains	72
	4.7 Conclusions and recommendations	73
	References	75
5	**Illegitimate Trade in Fashion and Technologies for Traceability and Supply Chain Protection** by *Iolanda D'Amato*	**79**
	5.1 Illegitimate trade and counterfeiting in fashion and luxury	79
	5.2 Countering illegitimate trade and protecting the legitimate supply chain	82
	5.3 Technologies for anti-counterfeiting and brand protection	84
	References	91
6	**Managing Circularity in Fashion** by *Francesca Romana Rinaldi and Elisabetta Amadei*	**93**
	6.1 The need for circularity	93
	6.2 Circular fashion: main principles and models	99
	References	113
7	**Collaborative Consumption in Fashion** by *Francesca Romana Rinaldi*	**115**
	7.1 Defining CFC	115
	7.2 CFC main business models in practice	116

	7.3 How can consumers benefit from CFC?	129
	7.4 Inhibitors to CFC from the consumer's point of view	130
	References	133

8 **The Purpose of Business, B-Corps and Benefit Corporations** 137
   by *Paolo Di Cesare, Eric Ezechieli, Samira Tasso, Silvia Zanazzi, Nicola Piccolo and Letizia Rigazzi*
   8.1 The shareholders paradigm 137
   8.2 B Corp & Benefit Corporation: the regenerative paradigm 138
   8.3 The B Corp model and the fashion industry: case studies 142
   References 150

9 **The Future of Fashion** 151
   by *Francesca Romana Rinaldi*
   9.1 How 4.0 technologies can disrupt and support sustainable fashion? 153
   9.2 An automated fashion industry? 161
   9.3 Towards fashion industry 2030 164
   References 173

Afterword by *Matteo Ward* 175

List of Boxes 179

The Authors 181

Foreword

by *Matteo Marzotto*

The textile and clothing supply chain has always had an extraordinary allure for me, mainly due to the high "intangible" content that characterizes the industry and can determine its success or failure.

The style, made up of volumes, colours, "hands", finishings, fits, details.

The communication, based on ideas, celebrity engagement, new or reinvigorated media and tools, interlinking with art and culture for inspiration, sometimes including provocative and challenging themes connected to dramatic socio-political events, sometimes referring to the past, reinterpreted in the light of contemporary creativity. On top of this heaps of passion and imagination.

Finally the brand, or company reputation, as the synthesis of all the elements.

The potential success, however, cannot become stable without the support of a rigorous and well-organized operating "machine" made of processes, times, calculations, percentages, contracts, laws, regulations, know-how, equipment, intelligence, hearts, hands and big investments: all extremely "tangible" components.

This continuous search for balance between the two key components of the fashion business – the "intangible" and the "tangible" – is governed by the mystery of human nature and its deepest aspects.

I believe that getting dressed cannot be reduced either today or in the future to "covering" one's body. In a world based on many freedoms, every human being chooses the most suitable outfit to wear according to their own sensitivity and perception, generally aiming to show the best personal image to the surrounding world.

I have often thought about this concept and continue to be fascinated by its apparent simplicity and huge implications. It is a concept that multiplies the various drivers towards success or failure.

Today we can state that sustainability is finally entering the scenario, as so powerfully described in this book: sustainability as a shared responsibility towards the environment, the planet's resources, mankind and all living beings. Sustainability thus comes onto the stage after decades of hesitation and mystification, after many words supported by very few facts. Commitment to sustainability will henceforth play a superstar role to become a fundamental element of the fashion industry and a factor in reshaping its future.

The "system" is changing radically and permanently. Fashion, which mirrors our essence, will be able to or will be forced to learn and implement new codes and new terms in its continuous and opportunistic evolution: environment, circularity, reuse, savings, transformation, optimization – relevant concepts impacting on the future of the world and of the human mankind. A huge challenge, a shift of paradigm where Italy can play a leading role, boosting responsible innovation due to its unique balance of competences and heritage.

Fashion Industry 2030 explores this radical and permanent shift towards a hopeful and better future.

I believe it is worth reading because of its rigorous approach – based on observation, figures, trends, market behaviours, best practices – and its brave assertion that things for the complex fashion pipeline have to change. Now and forever.

List of Acronyms

5G	Fifth Generation
AI	Artificial Intelligence
AR	Augmented Reality
B2B	Business to Business
B2C	Business to Consumer
B2G	Business to Government
BIA	B Impact Assessment
BRS	Business Requirement Specifications
C2C	Cradle2Cradle
CCBDA	Core Component Business Document Assembly
CFC	Collaborative Fashion Consumption
COGS	Cost of Goods Sold
CSR	Corporate Social Responsibility
DJSI	Dow Jones Sustainability Indices
EAN	European Article Number
EPC	Electronic Product Code
GF	Garment and Footwear
GOTS	Global Organic Textile Standard
ID	Identity
ILO	International Labour Organization
IoT	Internet of Things
ITC	International Trade Centre
LCA	Life Cycle Assessment
LDCs	Less Developed Countries
LEED	Leadership in Energy and Environmental Design
LISC	Legitimate Illegitimate Supply Chain
LLC	Limited Liability Company

LOHAS®	Lifestyle of Health and Sustainability
MBDC	McDonough Braungart Design Chemistry
MFA	Multi-Fibre Arrangement
NFC	Near-Field Communication
NGO	Non-Governmental Organization
NMI	Natural Marketing Institute
OECD	Organization for Economic Co-operation and Development
P2P	Peer to Peer
R&D	Research and Development
REACH	Registration, Evaluation, Authorisation and Restriction of Chemicals
RFID	Radio Frequency Identification
SBT	Science-Based Targets
SLCA	Strategic Life Cycle Assessment
UN	United Nations
UN/CEFACT	United Nations Centre for Trade Facilitation and Electronic Business
UNECE	United Nations Economic Commission for Europe
VR	Virtual Reality

Introduction

by *Francesca Romana Rinaldi*

Let's imagine the fashion industry in 2030. It won't be the same as today simply because of the sustainability pressures it faces.

Key data highlight the need for an immediate change.

At the G7 Summit that took place in 2019 at Biarrits (France), 32 major brands signed the "Fashion Pact", a document aimed at aligning the fashion industry with the UN Sustainable Development Goals (SDGs) to focus action on three gaps related to "climate", "biodiversity" and "oceans" with objectives drawn on the Science-Based Targets (SBT) Initiative.

For instance, 20% of the industry is now committing to net-zero carbon emissions by 2050 and the use of 100% renewable energy across own operations with the ambition to incentivize implementation of renewables in all high impact manufacturing processes along the entire supply chain by 2030 and eliminating the use of single use plastics (in both B2B and B2C packaging) by 2030. Is this enough?

The tremendous boom in clothing consumption will generate big increases in the use of resources and in the generation of waste. This needs to be managed. On the other hand, we can foresee that the demand of consumers interested in sustainability will rise: voices asking for sustainable fashion will become more mainstream. This consumer segment is influential and will therefore always be relevant for fashion companies.

The book *Fashion Industry 2030 – Reshaping the Future through Sustainability and Responsible Innovation* supports the thesis that an urgent and radical change is needed, both on the demand side and the supply side.

Consumers interested in sustainability will influence other segments by asking for more information, as they already do. Brands will be accustomed to explaining who made their products – and how and where they were made. Those same brands will have to develop new business models based on a value proposition that integrates ethics, aesthetics and innovation as fashion sustainability becomes a widely publicized issue.

This thesis has been partially discussed in the book *The Responsible Fashion Company*. Long-term economic balance in a company can only be achieved by incorporating economic short-term objectives, which are essential for the remuneration of capital and labour. Other non-economic objectives include the relationship with the environment, society, culture, the media, institutions, legislation and, most of all, the perspective of values and ethics.

Today, applying a multi-stakeholder approach for the integration of ethics and aesthetics may not be enough: there is a new need to reshape business models through responsible innovation.

This book investigates changes in the fashion industry towards sustainability and responsible innovation. The different chapters will focus on the key drivers that are propelling the industry towards the 4th Industrial Revolution. They answer the following questions:

- What can the various stakeholders do in order to speed up responsible innovation?
- How can consumers interested in sustainability contribute to this change?
- What will be the role of traceability, transparency, circularity, collaborative consumption, Benefit Corporations?
- How can technologies catalyse this change?

Key contributions by opinion leaders (company CEOs and entrepreneurs, institutions, associations, journalists, activists, etc.) are included. Among the many interviews conducted, some have been incredibly inspiring – for instance that with Nino Cerruti, in the Biella industrial district, cradle of high-quality textiles, located not so far away from the Italian fashion capital. Mr. Cerruti, who represents the third generation of one of the few companies still able to control the complete cycle of wool, from the Australian sheep to the Parisian catwalks, stated during an exclusive interview for this book:

> I think that the word *sustainable* is highly inflated and polluted and does not give the consumer the expected guarantee of meaning. For this reason, we need to start by giving this connotation a new definition that should be in relation to

the actual level of quality and to the value that is connected to the aesthetical content. Only in this way can we give due respect back to fashion and textiles.
Nino Cerruti, President of Lanificio F.lli Cerruti and Founder of Cerruti 1881

This is exactly the starting point: the word 'sustainability' must take on new meaning.

This empirical, case-oriented and interview-based approach will help explain how responsible innovation must be seen not only as a driver to update business models, but also as the only way to ensure medium- and long-term economic sustainability.

Chapter 1 starts with a topical debate on fashion companies and their important social role; the idea that the integration of ethics and aesthetics may not be enough is also discussed. Then, the concept of responsible innovation is introduced.

In Chapter 2, the characteristics of consumers interested in sustainability are analysed, exploring the many definitions of this consumer segment, the various clusters in existence and the specific communication tools to narrate sustainability in fashion, according to the different consumers' expectations.

In Chapter 3, Porter's Value Chain linear model is reinterpreted towards a 'Renewed Fashion Value Chain' model to introduce the business models that will be available in the fashion industry by 2030: this is the core chapter that links the whole book together.

Chapter 4's focus is on transparency and traceability for sustainable value chains in the fashion industry: their role as crucial enablers of more responsible production and consumption patterns is examined.

Chapter 5 is dedicated to technologies for traceability and supply chain protection, with a key focus on anti-counterfeiting.

Chapter 6 looks at how to manage circularity in fashion. The findings of the most updated reports on circular textiles and clothing are presented, together with a discussion of best practices underlying the opportunities and challenges of circularity in fashion.

Chapter 7 describes the opportunities of Collaborative Fashion Consumption (CFC). It presents the main business models and positive environmental effects and challenges of CFC (i.e. rental, subscription-rental and recommerce), following discussion of best practices.

Chapter 8 focuses on the description of the B-Corp certification and of the Benefit Corporation legal form. The case studies provide the reader with concrete examples of how some key players in the fashion industry have developed effective and innovative ways of incorporating sustainability principles into their everyday business practices.

Chapter 9 discusses the future of fashion towards 2030 and presents the point of view of several opinion leaders. Emerging technologies, such as wearables, blockchain, IoT, Augmented Reality (AR), Virtual Reality (VR), 3D printing, robotics, Artificial Intelligence (AI) and machine learning are discussed. These elements are driving the industry towards the 4th Industrial Revolution. Some open questions will be then presented at the end of our journey across the different drivers of change:

1. Which are the technologies that will disrupt more the industry and will drive business models towards a higher sustainability in fashion? Is blockchain a buzzword or it will really be the 'internet of the future'?
2. How is automation going to transform economies and the workforce?

To sum up, by 2030 the chances are high that some new rules of the game will reshape the business models of successful companies in the fashion industry:

1. Having traceable and transparent value chains.
2. Involving the consumer in a take-make-remake model to prolong product life.
3. Reading and interpreting data so that technologies can augment human creativity.
4. Granting consumer centricity, engagement and inclusivity.
5. Going from products to services.
6. Making profits without harming the environment or society.

By 2030, fashion companies will try to achieve 100% transparency and traceability. They will involve the consumers in their circular value chains, giving them many options to prolong the life of the product.

Fashion companies will put consumers' needs much more at the centre through product customization, on-demand collections, the omnichannel approach, transmedia storytelling and one-to-one communication. Thanks to AI it will be possible to craft effective user experiences, where all stakeholders will be active in the fashion value chains so the industry will be much more inclusive.

Introduction

Fashion companies will go from producing and distributing products to offering more personalized services such as repairing, renting and recommerce. In a nutshell, fashion companies of the future will be integrating aesthetics, ethics and responsible innovation.

Credits

This book is the result of the personal interest, as well as the academic and professional research, of the author. The introduction and Chapters 1, 2, 3, 7 (Chapter 7 was written with support from Accenture) and 9 were written by Francesca Romana Rinaldi; Chapter 4 was written by Maria Teresa Pisani; Chapter 5 was written by Iolanda D'Amato; Chapter 6 was written by Francesca Romana Rinaldi in collaboration with Elisabetta Amadei; Chapter 8 was written by the Nativa team composed of Paolo Di Cesare, Eric Ezechieli, Samira Tasso, Silvia Zanazzi, Nicola Piccolo and Letizia Rigazzi.

Acknowledgements

A special acknowledgement goes to those who have contributed to generating ideas for the book.

I would like to thank Prof. Salvo Testa from giving me guidance during my whole career. Thanks to Prof. Emanuela Prandelli for letting me discuss with many students about responsible innovation at MAFED and Prof. Paola Varacca Capello for sharing her suggestions and being my reviewer. Thanks to Prof. Guido Corbetta for having given me the opportunity to start teaching.

A special acknowledgement goes to Matteo Marzotto e Matteo Ward for writing the Foreword of the book. Many thanks to Andrea Ruzzi and Paola Sironi from Accenture for the support in writing Chapter 7 on Collaborative Fashion Consumption.

A special thanks goes to all the people who have believed in the project and dedicated their time and attention during meetings, projects and interviews, in particular: Nino Cerruti, Marina Spadafora, Erika Andreetta, Albert Candiani, Simon Giuliani, Danielle Arzaga, Yannick Meijers, Varonica Tonini e Livia Mazzoni. Francois Souchet, Enrica Arena, Silvia

Giovanardi, Anna Fiscale, Chantal Marchetti and the entire Progetto Quid team, Eva Engelen, Enea Roveda and Tommaso Perrone, Iolanda D'Amato, Eric Ezechieli, Heinz Zeller, Orsola de Castro, Michelandelo Pistoletto, Anne-Ro Klevant Groen, Giorgio Ravasio, Isabella Tonelli, Emanuele Micheli, Fabio Foglia, Prof. Luigi Proserpio, Niccolò Desenzani, Nicola Giuggioli, Maria Teresa Pisani, Maria Benedetta Francesconi, Giusy Cannone, Simone Ubertino Rosso, Daniele Denegri and the entire Green Media Lab team, Mihela Hladin Wolfe, Yannick Meijers, Gianluca Pandolfo, Louise Brierley, Mario Campori, Stefano Bassi and the whole Patagonia team.

Thanks to Sara Sozzani Maino, Nicoletta Spolini and Elisa Pervinca Bellini and the whole Vogue Talents team.

Thanks also to the Bocconi students for providing food for thought, especially Michela Agarossi and Elisa Mora. Thanks to Sara Zanella and Olga Yanovska Bianchi.

Thanks to Erica Corbellini and Stefania Saviolo for their support.

Thanks to the MFI students of the Master in Fashion Direction, Brand & Business Management - Sustainability Management Track.

Thanks to Piero Jacomoni for inspiring me as an entrepreneur.

Thanks to Rossella Ravagli and Alessandra Guffanti for keeping alive a fruitful discussion about a more sustainable future for the industry.

Thanks to Alberto Sanna for letting me find out again what it means to be an activist for environment and society.

A special thanks to Liuba Napoli, Valentina Perissinotto, Lucia Paladino, Elena Cardin for giving me continuous support.

Thanks to Cinzia Facchi and the whole Egea team.

Thanks to Elena Riva, Flavia Bleu, Giulia Minola and the whole Visualmade team (http://www.visualmade.it) for designing the visual of the Renewed Fashion Value Chain and making the booktrailer.

Thanks also to Tiziano Guardini, Progetto Quid, WRÅD and Fashion Revolution for providing the images and videos for the booktrailer (https://www.youtube.com/watch?v=WGlcKLhPX4g).

Thanks to Francesca Mariani (www.francescamariani.com), best friend, artist and illustrator, who created the book cover.

Thanks to my friends and my family who supported me all the time.

1 The Relevance of Responsible Innovation in Fashion

by *Francesca Romana Rinaldi*

Buy less, choose well, make it last.
Vivienne Westwood

In recent decades, global interest in sustainability has been increasing dramatically, including in the world of fashion.
As we move towards 2030, the word sustainability takes on new meanings and key drivers are reshaping the fashion industry towards the 4th Industrial Revolution. Among these are traceability and transparency, circularity and collaborative consumption.

1.1 Fashion industry and sustainability: synonyms or oxymoron?

Fashion is one of the largest industries in the world economy. Unfortunately it is also the second most polluting industry after oil, with heavy negative social and environmental impacts.[1]

The main social risks for a fashion firm relate to labour and human rights, such as freedom of association, equal opportunities and no child labour; governance, anti-corruption and fair practices, such as fair competition; society and community development, the impact of the organization on social systems of the communities in which it operates; product- and consumer-related responsibility, which includes issues such as health and safety of consumers, information and labelling, marketing and privacy;

---

[1] UNECE, 2017.

relationship with suppliers, such as compliance with payment deadlines, or the enforcement of codes of conduct.[2]

Two important categories of the environmental impact of textile production and processing are related to the discharge of pollutants and consumption of water and energy.[3]

For example, 19% of all insecticides and 9% of all pesticides are used on cotton.[4] Producing 1kg of cotton (a pair of jeans) requires up to 20,000 litres of water.[5] Approximately 25% of chemicals manufactured globally are applied in the textile industry.[6]

Workers in the textile industry are exposed to chemicals that are linked to several kinds of cancers, including brain cancer, lung cancer and stomach cancer. Chemical contact with skin and inhalation can lead to other serious health effects, while exposure to noise also represents a serious risk to workers.[7]

In recent decades, the search for low-cost labour and proximity to sources of raw materials have favoured the rapid transformation of supply chains. As a result, firms have endured increasing pressure from governments, consumers and NGOs to extend Corporate Social Responsibility (CSR) practices to their production lines, including not only first-tier but also second- and third-tier suppliers as well.

The ongoing financial and economic crisis in Western countries has accelerated the debate on CSR, to the extent that today it is considered a necessary condition for competitiveness. For firms in the fashion industry in particular, an important opportunity to regain the confidence of consumers is evident: to restore their value systems and business models by making quality and product innovation the central focus once again.[8]

At a global level, the fashion sector has embraced a variety of different business models and approaches: fast fashion versus the traditional model, volumes versus quality, global supply chains versus short supply chains, standardization versus craftsmanship of the product. Globalization has led to the fragmentation of the supply chain, displacing a great part of

---

[2] UNECE, 2017.
[3] UNEP, 2014.
[4] Cheung *et al.*, 2006.
[5] Camargue, 2006.
[6] Greenpeace, 2013.
[7] Oecotextiles, 2013.
[8] Rinaldi and Testa, 2014.

the manufacturing that was originally carried out locally to developing countries. Given this variety of business models and approaches, the fashion industry is now experiencing a change in key success factors towards quality and responsibility.

1.2 Increasing interest in CSR

The reasons for increasing interest in CSR are common to a wide range of sectors and concern a number of changes which have taken place in terms of both demand and supply: the awareness of the scarcity of our planet's resources; the evolution of the consumer; the delocalization of production and the globalization of the supply chain; the proliferation of scandals related to the use of child labour and the lack of compliance with the working conditions set down by the ILO (International Labour Organization), a specialist UN agency that pursues the promotion of social justice and of internationally acknowledged human rights, with particular reference to employment rights; the increase of multi-stakeholder associations;[9] the increased speed and low cost of information dissemination thanks to computer technology, the internet and social networks.[10]

The result of all these factors is the growing importance of the concepts of traceability and transparency. The latter is not only requested by consumers, but also by financial markets: this is demonstrated by the creation of stock indexes like the Dow Jones Sustainability Indices (DJSI) that only list firms that can show they meet certain environmental requirements. The desire to be included in these indexes has led to the development of social and ecological practices, especially among the big listed firms.[11]

On an empirical basis, investing in CSR can activate a virtuous cycle and plays a significant role in enhancing a firm's value.[12] Investing in CSR activities can enhance operating efficiency,[13] product market gains,[14] im-

---

[9] For example, the Ethical Trading Initiative, the Fair Wear Foundation and the Worker Rights Consortium.
[10] Rancati, 2007.
[11] Rinaldi and Testa, 2014.
[12] Malik, 2015.
[13] Porter and Kramer, 2002; Saiia *et al.*, 2003; Brammer and Millington, 2005.
[14] Menon and Kahn, 2003.

prove employee productivity,[15] bring some capital market benefits,[16] improve risk management[17] and earnings quality.[18] Finally, investing in CSR activities can also improve a company's reputation and increase current and potential new employees' motivation.

1.3 From shareholder to shared value

Sustainability (economic, environmental and social) implies responsible behaviour, intended as the creation of value for stakeholders as well as for shareholders. The word *sustainability* would be meaningless without a new way of understanding value: in the past 'creating value' in a firm simply meant making higher profits than the competitors and dividends to distribute to those providing the capital. Today the idea of 'shareholder value maximization' in the short term is no longer sufficient and is radically changing into a concept that leads to the affirmation of new business models.[19]

Porter and Kramer, in their article 'Creating Shared Value', published in the *Harvard Business Review* (2011), stated: 'The solution lies in the principle of shared value, which involves value for society by addressing its needs and challenges. Businesses must reconnect firm success with social progress. Shared value is a new way to achieve economic success.' Thus, sustainability may increase the chances of survival for firms in the medium to long term and may become a source of competitive advantage.[20]

The innovation achieved thanks to business models founded on responsibility is based on the creation of shared value: the increase in value for shareholders will then be a direct consequence of the increase in value for all stakeholders. However, many firms think about CSR as a mere public relations tool aimed at strengthening their reputation (cost logic). Porter and Kramer (2006) argue that it is still the case for many firms.

---

[15] Tuzzolino and Armandi, 1981; Trevino and Nelson, 2004; Valentine and Fleischman, 2008.
[16] Godfrey, 2005; Dhaliwal *et al.*, 2012.
[17] Richardson and Welker, 2001; Dhaliwal *et al.*, 2011; Husted, 2005.
[18] Chih *et al.*, 2008; Hong and Andersen, 2011; Kim *et al.*, 2012.
[19] Magatti, 2011.
[20] Porter and Kramer, 2011.

CSR is seen as a public relations tool, rather than a value-creating process in its own right, whose goal is to assist manufacturing firms in achieving sustainability [...] some firms have claimed to pursue CSR, but in fact have only used contributions to social objectives as a mechanism for carrying on profit maximizing operations. Profit is an integral part and a tangible way of evaluating a firm's growth; however, it is not the only objective.[21]

Sustainability's journey from the cost logic to business logic is obligatory for creating shared value and provides at least two fundamental elements: dialogue with a multiplicity of stakeholders and CSR initiatives connected to the core business.

A journey around sustainable fashion discussed in the scientific literature is presented in Box 1.

Box 1 Sustainable fashion discussed in the scientific literature

> The first journals that aimed to define the meaning of social responsibility in the fashion industry as a 'context' were published during the 1990s. According to Littrell and Dickson's (1999) study: 'social responsibility places major emphasis on day-to-day actions within a business as related to product sourcing, employee treatment, and working conditions'.[22]
> The full focus on the industry arrived with Dickson and Eckman (2006):[23] the authors conducted a survey to the members of the International Textile and Apparel (T&A) Association to define the concept 'socially responsible' among T&A educators.
> A socially responsible T&A business could be defined as: 'an orientation encompassing the environment, its people, the apparel/textile products made and consumed, and the systematic impact that production, marketing, and consumption of these products and their component parts has on multiple stakeholders and the environment. A philosophy that balances ethics/morality with profitability, which is achieved through accountability-based business decisions and strategies ... [and] a desire for outcomes that positively affect, or do very little harm to, the world and its people'.[24]

---

[21] Porter and Kramer, 2006.
[22] Dickson and Littrell, 1996, p. 6.
[23] Dickson and Eckman, 2006.
[24] Dickson and Eckman, 2006, p. 188.

Dickson and colleagues[25] then focused on the specific issues related to social responsibility within fashion, such as resource consumption, pollution, health and safety, consumer wellbeing, human rights and product quality and affordability. They proposed an original model of social responsibility for the T&A industry. Their model shows the different results that can arise from a three-way approach to the environment, people and systems by adopting a philosophy and implementing actions that work in favour of ethics and of economy.

According to the authors, in order for a firm in the T&A sector to be considered responsible, it needs to be moved by a philosophy that balances ethics and profit, considering its social responsibility in everyday decisions; it must adopt an approach aimed at a systematic assessment of environmental and social sustainability; and it must constantly strive towards improvement and to the reduction of its socio-environmental impact at a global level. The areas in which firms must focus more to improve their sustainable results are represented by: consumer welfare and safety, product quality, wellbeing and safety of workers, reduction of pollution and of the consumption of natural resources and respect for human rights.

More recently, the scientific literature on the fashion industry has been examining innovative and sustainable business models, which ties in with the focus of this book.

For instance, an article published in 2016 in the *Journal of Business Ethics* explores the relationship among business model innovation, corporate sustainability and organizational values within the fashion industry. Pedersen *et al.*, through the analysis of 492 survey responses from managers belonging to the Swedish fashion industry, found out that companies with innovative business models are more likely to address CSR and that business model innovation and CSR are typically found in organizations rooted in values of flexibility and discretion as fundamental principles guiding the organization. The study also confirms a positive relationship between the core organizational values and financial performance.[26]

Another article published in 2017 in Business Horizons discusses about innovative and sustainable business models in the fashion industry. Todeschini *et al.*[27] combined a systematic review of the literature with empirical research comprised of six interviews with specialists in sustainability, business model innovation, and the fashion industry, along with eight case studies on innovative fashion startups defined as 'born sustainable': they concluded that "there is still a gap between what theory argues and the levels of environmental and social sustainability realized when theory is put into practice".

---

[25] Dickson *et al.*, 2009.
[26] Pedersen *et al.*, 2016.
[27] Todeschini *et al.*, 2017.

1.4 The Responsible Fashion Company

The goal to make a more specific consumer-centric and multi-stakeholder model was defined in *The Responsible Fashion Company*.[28] The book offers guidelines for CSR managers operating in the industry to promote more responsible behaviour of their firms towards the different stakeholders. It introduces a new management model based on three variables that fashion firms have to manage better in the short and long term: ethics, aesthetics and profitability. The three variables connect the fashion firm with different contexts: the environmental and social contexts are common to many other sectors. Other more industry-specific contexts are added to fashion: media, artistic, cultural and territorial, regulatory and institutional context (Figure 1).

Figure 1   New model for responsibility in fashion: the stakeholders and the dimensions of context

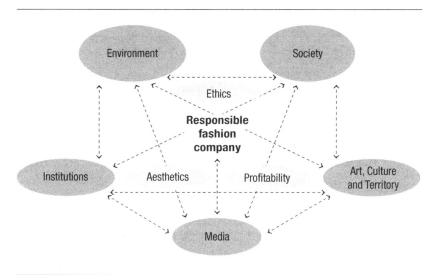

Source: Rinaldi and Testa (2014).

---

[28] Rinaldi and Testa, 2014.

In brief, the responsible fashion firm is willing to:[29]

- respect the environment by using raw materials with a lower impact to the territory and its workers (for example, preferring organic cotton, flax and hemp instead of traditional cotton) and optimizing the consumption of the other resources used in production and distribution (energy, water);
- protect the social territory, workers and consumers, while respecting International Labour Organization (ILO) principles and ensuring a qualitatively satisfactory product;
- increase the consumer's involvement through communication and convey a positive message with authenticity and transparency in order to influence their behaviour, for example educating them to take care of the product and making them more mindful of the importance of their actions;
- support the culture, landscape and territory in which it is located through concrete and lasting initiatives;
- comply with the regulations on environmental and social protection, but voluntarily adopt a proactive attitude in respect of more advanced standards, such as environmental and social certifications;
- adopt an ethical attitude towards employees by giving a fair salary, to respect the human dignity of the collaborators and consumers, to respect codes of conduct, to contribute to collective social and civil progress, and to that of the community of reference, to ensure that aesthetics is a bearer of positive values and to trigger a mechanism of responsibility in the value chain.

1.5 Responsible innovation: the missing ingredient!

Talking about sustainable fashion has become commonplace, not least because the horrific Rana Plaza disaster in Bangladesh and other sweatshop accidents have been a long-overdue wake-up call to the industry. But most

---

[29] Rinaldi and Testa, 2014.

discussions on this topic still lack adequate knowledge and a shared language.

This is not just about bamboo and hemp clothing. It is not just about having a conscience. The big potential here is to integrate ethics, aesthetics and innovation across all the activities of the value chain.

In accordance with recent trends in the scientific literature,[30] this book supports the thesis that responsible innovation is needed to make a truly responsible fashion company.

Responsible innovation is considered as an innovation related to the product, service or, more comprehensively, to the business model that is able to reduce the impact on the environment across the firm processes and to build a better balance with the people involved in the economic and non-economic activity of the company.

The complexity related to responsible fashion applied to the value chain is very high and requires relevant investments of resources and time, but the number of companies now reshaping, or willing to gradually reshape their business models towards sustainability are not just a few.

References

Brammer, S. & Millington, A. (2005). 'Corporate reputation and philanthropy: An empirical analysis'. *Journal of Business Ethics*, 61, 29–44.

Camargue, F. (2006). 'Drought in the Mediterranean'. *WWF Policy Proposals*.

Cheung, K., Sirur, G. & Anderdon, J. (2006). 'Agrochemical service. Fungicides', *Cropnosis*, 1-41.

Chih, H., Shen, C. & Kang, F. (2008). 'Corporate social responsibility, investor protection, and earnings management: Some international evidence'. *Journal of Business Ethics*, 79(1/2), 179–198.

Commission of the European Communities (2001). 'Green Paper. 'Promoting a European Framework for Corporate Social Responsibility' (available on the website https://www.eea.europa.eu/policy-documents/com-2001-366-final-green).

Commission of the European Communities (2002). 'Corporate Social Responsibility – Main Issues', *MEMO/02/153*, Brussels. http://europa.eu/rapid/press-release_MEMO-02-153_en.htm.

---

[30] Pedersen & Andersen, 2015; Pedersen *et al.*, 2016; Todeschini *et al.*, 2017.

Dhaliwal, D.S., Li, O. Z., Tsang, A. & Yang, Y.G. (2011). 'Voluntary nonfinancial disclosure and the cost of equity capital: The initiation of corporate social responsibility reporting', *The Accounting Review*, 86(1), 59–100.

Dhaliwal, D.S., Radhakrishnan, S., Tsang, A. & Yang, Y.G. (2012). 'Nonfinancial disclosure and analyst forecast accuracy: International evidence on corporate social responsibility disclosure', *The Accounting Review*, 87(3), 723–759.

Dickson, M.A. & Littrell, M.A. (1996). 'Socially responsible behaviour: Values and attitudes of the alternative trading organisation consumer', *Journal of Fashion Marketing and Management: An International Journal*, 1(1), 50–69.

Dickson, M.A., Loker, S. & Eckman, M. (2009). *Social Responsibility in the Global Apparel Industry*. New York, Fairchild Books.

European Commission (2011). 'Corporate social responsibility: A new definition, a new agenda for action', http://europa.eu/rapid/press-release_MEMO-11-730_en.htm.

Garriga, E. & Melé, D. (2004). 'Corporate social responsibility theories: Mapping the territory', *Journal of Business Ethics*, 53(1), 51–71.

Godfrey, P.C. (2005). 'The relationship between corporate philanthropy and shareholder wealth: A risk management perspective', *Academy of Management Review*, 30, 777–798.

Greenpeace (2013), 'Chemicals substitution in textile industry: implementing chemical policies into the textile supply chain' (available on the website https://www.greenpeace.org/china/Global/china/publications/others/2013/20130325-GP-ENG.pdf).

Hong, Y. & Andersen, M.L. (2011). 'The relationship between corporate social responsibility and earnings management: An exploratory study', Journal of Business Ethics, 104, 461–471.

Husted, B.W. (2005). 'Risk management, real options, and corporate social responsibility', *Journal of Business Ethics*, 60, 175–183.

Johnson, Kim K.P. et al. (2013). 'Trends in research addressing fashion and social responsibility', *Journal of Global Fashion Marketing*, 4(3), 145–157.

Khurana, K. & Ricchetti, M. (2016). 'Two decades of sustainable supply chain management in the fashion business, an appraisal', *Journal of Fashion Marketing and Management: An International Journal*, 20(1), 89–104.

Kim, Y., Park, M.S. & Wier, B. (2012). 'Is earnings quality associated with corporate social responsibility?', *The Accounting Review*, 87(3), 761–796.

Köksal, D., Strähle, J., Müller, M. & Freise, M. (2017). 'Social Sustainable supply chain management in the textile and apparel industry – a literature review', *Sustainability*, 9, 100.

Magatti, M. (ed.) (2011). *Verso nuovi modelli di business*. Milan, Bruno Mondadori.

Malik, M. (2015). 'Value-enhancing capabilities of CSR: A brief review of contemporary literature', *Journal of Business Ethics*, 127(2), 419–438.

Menon, S. & Kahn, B.E. (2003). 'Corporate sponsorships of philanthropic activities: When do they impact perception of sponsor brand?', *Journal of Consumer Psychology*, 13(3), 316–327.
Oecotextiles (2013). https://oecotextiles.wordpress.com/tag/greenhouse-gas.
Pedersen, E.R.G. & Andersen, K.R. (2015). 'Sustainability innovators and anchor draggers: A global expert study on sustainable fashion', *Journal of Fashion Marketing & Management*, 19(3), 315–327.
Pedersen, E.R.G., Gwozdz, W. & Hvass, K.K. (2016). 'Exploring the relationship between business model innovation, corporate sustainability, and organisational values within the fashion industry' *Journal of Business Ethics*, https://doi.org/10.1007/s10551-016-3044-7.
Perrini, F. & Tencati, A. (2008). *Corporate Social Responsibility. Un nuovo approccio strategico alla gestione d'impresa*. Milan, Egea.
Pogutz, S. (2007). 'Responsabilità sociale d'impresa e pratica aziendale: una rassegna delle principali esperienze', in Romano Benini (ed.), *L'impresa responsabile e la comunità intraprendente. Responsabilità sociale, territorio e piccole imprese in rete*. Avellino, Halley.
Porter, M.E. & Kramer, M.R. (2002). 'The competitive advantage of corporate philanthropy', *Harvard Business Review*, 80, 5–16.
Porter, M.E. & Kramer, M.R. (2006). 'Strategy and society: The link between corporate social responsibility and competitive advantage', *Harvard Business Review*, 84(12), 78-92.
Porter, M.E. & Kramer, M.R. (2011). 'Creating shared value', *Harvard Business Review*, 89(1–2), 62–77.
Rancati, E. (2007). 'Il tempo nelle imprese orientate alla concorrenza', in S.M. Brondoni (edited by), *Market-Driven Management e mercati globali*. Tourin, Giappichelli.
Richardson, A. & Welker, M. (2001). 'Social disclosure, financial disclosure and the cost of equity capital', *Accounting, Organizations and Society*, 26, 597–616.
Rinaldi, F.R. & Testa S. (2014). *The Responsible Fashion Company*. Abingdon, Greenleaf Publishing – Routledge.
Saiia, D.H., Carroll, A. B. & Buchholtz, A. K. (2003). 'Philanthropy as strategy: When corporate charity "begins at home"', *Business and Society*, 42, 169–201.
Todeschini, B.V., Cortimiglia, M.N., Callegaro-de-Menezes, D., & Ghezzi, A. (2017). Innovative and sustainable business models in the fashion industry: Entrepreneurial drivers, opportunities, and challenges. *Business Horizons*, 60(6), 759-770.
Trevino, L.K. & Nelson, K.A. (2004). *Managing Business Ethics: Straight Talk about How to Do it Right* (3rd ed.). New York, John Wiley and Sons.
Tuzzolino, F. & Armandi, B.R. (1981). 'A need-hierarchy framework for assessing corporate social responsibility', *Academy of Management Review*, 6(1), 21–28.

UNECE (2017). 'Textile4SDG12: Transparency in textile value chains in relation to the environmental, social and human health impacts of parts, components and production processes', https://www.unece.org/fileadmin/DAM/uncefact/UNECE_Research_Paper_Traceability_for_Sustainable_Clothing_Nov_2017_FINAL.pdf.

Valentine, S. & Fleischman, G. (2008). 'Ethics programs, perceived corporate social responsibility and job satisfaction', *Journal of Business Ethics*, 77, 159–172.

2   One Size Doesn't Fit All

by *Francesca Romana Rinaldi*

> *Change is coming, whether you like it or not.*
> Greta Thunberg

Consumers interested in sustainability pursue a lifestyle based on attention to their own health and that of the planet. Consequently, when shopping, these consumers choose carefully, are aware of the importance of quality and the origin of products. This chapter explores many definitions of this consumer segment, the various clusters in existence and the specific communication tools to narrate sustainability in fashion, according to different consumer expectations. Companies should adopt a customized strategy: tone of voice, content, media and channels to communicate sustainability should be adapted in accordance with the consumers' type.

2.1   Defining the consumers interested in sustainability

Consumers interested in sustainability are growing at global level. A BCG ad hoc study for Altagamma based on a survey of 12,000 luxury consumers in ten countries declared that 'social wearers' generated €23 billion in 2016.[1] By 2030, Global Fashion Agenda and BCG forecast that the fashion industry could generate €160 billion thanks to sustainable practices.[2] On the basis of these data, it can be affirmed that consumers interested about sustainability represent today quite a relevant 'niche'.

---

[1] BCG–Altagamma, 2017.
[2] Global Fashion Agenda and BCG, 2017.

From cultural creatives to LOHAS®

Cultural creatives, social wearers, ethical consumers, green consumer, LOHAS® (Lifestyle of Health and Sustainability) consumers: those are just some of the names given to people interested in sustainability – including interest in sustainable fashion.

The first definition of consumers interested in sustainability was given during the mid-1990s by the American sociologist Paul Ray and the psychologist Sherry Anderson in their book *Cultural Creatives*.[3]

The values that distinguish Cultural Creatives' lifestyle are mainly: integrity, authenticity, spirituality, ecological sensitivity, the quality of social relations, altruism and curiosity.

Limited to a minority of the American population up until the mid-1990s, the Cultural Creatives experienced a steady growth, representing in 2008 about 35% of Americans, which equates to about 80 million adults.[4]

The expansion of the Cultural Creatives segment has captured the interest of researchers and companies, who understood that the traditional methods of segmentation were no longer sufficient to describe the market. Consumer lifestyle and psychographic characteristics started to be used then as a proxy for its purchasing behaviour.

In 2002 the Natural Marketing Institute (NMI)[5] published a new market segmentation based on attitudes towards sustainability, from which emerged a new cluster that was called LOHAS®, that at the beginning of the millennium was about 20% of the overall U.S. population.[6]

There is no doubt that there is a correspondence between Cultural Creatives and LOHAS®. However, a distinction must be made: the expression Cultural Creatives defines a group of a sociocultural nature; the term LOHAS®, on the other hand, refers to individuals as consumers.

With its research on the U.S. population, the NMI has identified five segments:[7]

- LOHAS®;
- Naturalites®;

---

[3] Ray and Anderson, 2000.
[4] http://culturalcreatives.org.
[5] NMI is an American consultancy and research institute specializing in the health and wellness sectors.
[6] www.nmisolutions.com.
[7] www.nmisolutions.com.

- Drifters®;
- Conventionals®;
- Unconcerneds®.

While the Unconcerneds® show no involvement in the responsibility, the Conventionals®, the Drifters® and the Naturalites® adopt sustainable measures but in a non-constant way or are driven by reasons of opportunistic nature.

LOHAS®, on the other hand, simultaneously seek personal, social and environmental wellbeing and actively engage in changing the world in which they live. The main characteristics are summed up in Table 1.

Table 1 Main characteristics of NMI consumer clusters

LOHAS®	NATURALITES®	DRIFTERS®	CONVENTIONALS®	UNCON-CERNEDS®
Personal and planetary health priority; sustainability is entrenched in lifestyle; haviest purchasers of "green"; early adopters & influencers.	Personal health drivers grater than planetary health; strong secondary target for natural/green consumer packaged goods brands.	Green followers; newer to the green marketplace; want to be seen as doing their part; in search of easy green changes.	Practical and rational; driven by cost savings; eco-benefits secondary.	Less concerned about the environment and society.

Source: https://www.nmisolutions.com/syndicated-data/segmentation-algorithms-a-panels/lohas-segmentation.

Although the data mentioned here refer to the U.S. market, the LOHAS® consumer segment has also spread to other countries in the world.

The LOHAS® lifestyle can be called 'hybrid': being LOHAS® means supporting technological evolution, enjoying nature, living a life always self-centred but also sharing with others. LOHAS® people are realistic but open to spiritual ideals.[8]

The total commitment of LOHAS® to sustainability is reflected in all consumption choices and can be summarized in five pillars: healthy life,

---

[8] Kreeb *et al.*, 2009, p. 310.

alternative medicine, personal development, green economy and social justice. The LOHAS® lifestyle and values are significantly influencing the way of doing business and consumption habits of a large portion of the population.[9]

Ernst & Young, in a 2008 study, considered three scenarios that trace possible LOHAS® developments:[10]

- Scenario 1 'Niche',
- Scenario 2 'Mainstream',
- Scenario 3 'Boom',

By 2030 the most probable scenario is the 'Boom', where LOHAS® becomes the dominant lifestyle: this scenario opens the way to reflection upon the opportunities for developing more sustainable new products in different categories, including in the fashion sector.

Especially after the Rana Plaza disaster (April 23, 2013), the level of involvement of the younger generation towards a more sustainable fashion industry is evident, also thanks to a global movement such as Fashion Revolution (Box 2).

Box 2 Engaging the younger generation in sustainable fashion

Fashion Revolution is a global movement that was created after the Rana Plaza disaster and that continues to grow, with more people calling for a fairer, safer, more transparent fashion industry. In April 2017 Fashion Revolution saw 2 million people engaging through events, posting on social media, viewing videos or downloading resources from the website. The hashtag was very simple #whomademyclothes. It was very true and catchy. Every time I buy a piece of clothing I ask, do I know who made it? If not, why don't I know? Why isn't there a transparent production chain, so that I can actually know where the cotton or the wool was sourced? How was it woven into a fabric or yarn? Who made it? Was the person who made it paid a fair amount? Was he/she working in a safe environment?

Fashion Revolution believes that the change has to be made by educating consumers, starting from a young age. For this reason they work a lot with schools to bring the message to younger people in order to make them realize that every time we spend our money, we cast a vote for the world that we want. We can be informed, we can be curious and find out which are the brands that are doing things properly.

---

[9] www.lohas.com.
[10] Ernst & Young, 2008.

In 2018, Fashion Revolution commissioned a survey of 5,000 people aged 16–75 in the five largest European markets, Germany, United Kingdom, France, Italy and Spain, to find out how supply-chain transparency and sustainability impacts on consumers' purchasing decisions when shopping for clothing, accessories and shoes. The survey was conducted as part of a baseline study in the 'Trade Fair, Live Fair' project. 'Trade Fair, Live Fair' is a three-year project funded by the European Commission and brings together 31 partners from the Fair Trade community across the EU, including Fashion Revolution, Fairtrade International, Fairtrade Foundation, World Fair Trade Organisation, Fair Trade Advocacy Office and many others.

The main results can be summarized as follows:

- A significant number of people consider social and environmental impacts when shopping, but the vast majority of people would like to learn more about where their clothes are made and who makes them, as well as what fashion brands are going to address social and environmental issues.
- The majority of people also think that governments have a crucial role to play in ensuring the clothes people buy are made sustainably. The majority of people also think that governments should be responsible for holding fashion brands to account for disclosing information about the way their products are made, what suppliers they are working with and how they're applying socially and environmentally responsible practices in their supply chains.
- When it comes to buying clothes, more people care about workers being paid fair, living wages and environmental protection than they do about clothes being produced locally or made without harming animals or using recycled materials.
- Consumers expect fashion brands to be more transparent by sharing detailed information about the factories where their clothes are made and the suppliers they use to source the materials, ingredients and components used in their clothes.

Source: Interview with Marina Spadafora, Country Coordinator, Fashion Revolution Italy, and Ipsos-Mori (2018).

2.2 Does one size fit all?

Although there is evidence of the presence of some global characteristics for consumers interested in sustainability, one size doesn't fit all. An exploratory study carried out in the Italian market[11] and published in *Econo-*

---

[11] The 206 respondents were Italian consumers interested in sustainability: they were involved though a network of Italian associations and communication agencies focused on sustainable fashion.

mia & Management,[12] the SDA Bocconi School of Management journal, made it possible to identify the significant differences among consumers interested in sustainability. A cluster analysis allowed the identification of four types (see Box 3 and Table 2) by using the Lifestyle Segmentation looking at Attitudes, Interests and Opinions:

- Fashion-driven: consumers who give great importance to aesthetics and little importance to responsibility;
- Balanced: consumers that seek a balance between responsibility and aesthetics;
- Radicals: subordinate aesthetics to responsibility;
- Value-driven: consumers who prioritize quality, price and durability.

Box 3 Main characteristics of consumers interested in sustainability in Italy

Fashion-driven consumers give great importance to aesthetics and little importance to responsibility. It is the segment least worried about animal welfare issues and also the one with the lowest number of vegetarians. For this cluster, however, quality and price are also important.
Balanced consumers, as their name suggests, seek a balance between responsibility and aesthetics and consider the style of a fashion product to be the first consideration, immediately followed by responsibility towards the planet and the people, while responsibility towards animals is considered less relevant. Furthermore, they mostly buy organic products or low food-miles: this is probably a group of consumers whose sense of responsibility has spread progressively from food to fashion, where in any case aesthetics still remains a priority. The subordination of the ethical aspect is also confirmed by the quantity of responsible clothing items owned.
Radicals subordinate aesthetics to responsibility, including in the choice of clothing. They are characterized by a low price sensitivity, give great importance to the protection of animals, a principle also respected in the food they eat. They have a strong sense of responsibility towards others, and make purchasing choices in favour of sustainable products.

---

[12] Rinaldi and Pandolfini, 2015.

Value-driven consumers are the smallest segment identified. For this consumer type, the features that really matter in buying a fashion product are quality, price and durability. Yet responsability – in particular respect for the environment – is considered more relevant than aesthetics. The relevance assumed by responsibility, also in terms of fashion, leads them to buy more responsible garments, although these still represent a minority compared to the entire wardrobe.

Source: Rinaldi and Pandolfini, 2015.

Table 2 Main characteristics of consumers interested in sustainability in Italy

AIO		Fashion-driver	Balanced	Radicals	Value-driven
Activities		Reading Social life Cooking	Travel Sport Culture Meeting friends	Volunteering Culture Reading Meeting friends	Reading Culture Meeting friends
Interests		Cooking Travel	Travel	Travel	Cooking Travel
Opinions	*Religion*	Poor practice	Strong spirituality	Weak interest, rational approach	Strong spirituality
	Medicine	Scepticism towards traditional medicine	Alternative medicine	Weak use of alternative medicine	Alternative medicine
	Family	Integration of work, family and friends for self-realization	Need for balance	Work as a form of self-realization	Need for balance

Source: Rinaldi and Pandolfini, 2015.

According to the characteristics of the different consumer segments, companies communicate differently: for example Fashion-driven consumers will never feel involved through static sustainability reports and it would rather be useful to communicate through emotional videos. On the other hand, companies could prefer to communicate to Balanced consumers through a mix of tools, such as section of the website, certifications and QRcode labelling. In addition, the language, tone of voice and content should be adapted in order to be relevant to the specific customer cluster.

To sum up, aesthetics remains a fundamental criterion for most consumers and there are segments with different predispositions for responsible purchasing, attributing a different priority to the aesthetic component rather than the ethical one. From this point of view, the group that offers the most opportunities is represented by the Balanced, who are looking for both sustainability and style. Fashion brands could therefore focus more on this segment in the future, constructing an offer that is consistent with the stylistic identity of the individual brands, while, at the same time, meeting the socio-environmental sustainability criteria assessed by consumers as priorities.

To improve the fashion industry by 2030 some challenges are clear:

- companies still did not explore in depth the psychographic characteristics and the renewed needs of consumers interested in sustainability, so the priority is to carry out a better LOHAS® market segmentation and analysis;
- companies often do not have sufficient sustainability content to communicate, so the priority is to improve their CSR performance, to meet the needs of the consumers interested in sustainability;
- companies do not properly convey the contents of their sustainability initiatives, so the priority is to implement some principles of sustainable communication.

The next section will focus on some relevant existing guidelines to effectively communicate sustainability content in fashion.

2.3 SDG 12 and sustainable communication in fashion

The Sustainable Development Goals (Figure 2) are the blueprint created by the United Nations (UN) to achieve a better and more sustainable future for all. They address global challenges including those related to poverty, inequality, climate, environmental degradation, prosperity, peace and justice.

SDG 12, 'Sustainable consumption and production', is about promoting resource and energy efficiency, sustainable infrastructure, providing access to basic services, green and decent jobs and a better quality of life for all. Its implementation helps to achieve overall development plans, reduce fu-

Figure 2 The UN Sustainable Development Goals 2030

Source: https://www.un.org/sustainabledevelopment/sustainable-development-goals.

ture economic, environmental and social costs, strengthen economic competitiveness and reduce poverty.

SDG 12.8 states that by 2030, we need to ensure that people everywhere have the relevant information and awareness for sustainable development and lifestyles in harmony with nature.

Thus, one of the aims of SDG 12 is educating consumers on sustainable consumption and lifestyles, providing them with adequate information through standards and labels and engaging in sustainable public procurement, among others.

Some key principles are therefore needed to communicate effectively sustainability contents to consumers that are interested about what is behind the product.

UN guidelines for providing product sustainability information

The One Planet Network brings together a global community helping to achieve SDG 12. One of six programmes under this network, the Consumer Information Programme gathers initiatives, knowledge tools and projects around the communication of product sustainability.

In this context, between June 2015 and October 2017, UN Environment and the International Trade Centre convened a working group comprising over 35 experts from various sectors and regions, which held several virtual meetings and one in-person workshop to develop the Guidelines for Providing Product Sustainabiltiy Information (the 'Guidelines'). Comments received from more than 90 organizations during a two-month global consultation were also vital to the development process. They have been road-tested by organizations from different sectors and regions in 2017.[13]

The Guidelines aim to set a common ground for reliable product sustainability information to consumers, providing value chain and public sector professionals with clear guidance on how to make effective, trustworthy claims to consumers, on product-related sustainability information, aiming to empower consumers to make informed sustainable choices (Box 4).

Information around the Guidelines is collected on the 'Product Sustainability Information Hub,[14] which has the objective to provide the network of the Consumer Information Programme with information and news on what is being developed on the topic.

Box 4 UN guidelines for providing product sustainability information[15]

The guidelines for providing product sustainability information propose two types of principles: the fundamental and the aspirational.

The '*fundamental principles*' describe the fundamental criteria on which sustainability claims must be based. The Guidelines request its users to comply with all of the fundamental principles, which seek to build and reinforce each other, and lay the foundations for the subsequent 'aspirational principles'.

Under each principle, guiding questions and examples are provided to help users understand and apply the principles' requirements.

---

[13] https://www.oneplanetnetwork.org.
[14] https://www.oneplanetnetwork.org/consumer-information-scp/product-sustainability-information-hub.
[15] See https://www.oneplanetnetwork.org/resource/guidelines-providing-product-sustainability-information.

The '*aspirational principles*' propose to provide product sustainability information to consumers in a dynamic process, in which consumers should be engaged. Not only should information be provided to them, but they should be consulted and interacted with, to better understand their information needs. These aspirational principles are for information providers to go beyond the fundamental principles and to continuously improve the ways in which they communicate to consumers. They are not compulsory to implement (when following the Guidelines), but all users should ultimately aspire to do so. The fundamental principles must not be abandoned or replaced by the aspirational principles (Figure 3).

Figure 3 The fundamental and aspirational principles of UN Guidelines providing product sustainability information

FUNDAMENTAL PRINCIPLES

RELIABILITY
Build your claims on a reliable basis
- Accurate and scientifically true
- Robust and consistent
- Substantiated data and assumptions

RELEVANCE
Talk about major improvements, in areas that matter
- Significant aspects ('hotspots') covered
- Not masking poor product performance, no burden shifting
- Genuine benefit which goes beyond legal compliance

CLARITY
Make the information useful for the consumer
- Exclusive and direct link between claim and product
- Explicit and easy to understand
- Limits of claim clearly stated

TRANSPARENCY
Satisfy the consumer's appetite for information, and do not hide
- Developer of the claim and provider of evidence published
- Traceability and generation of claim (methods, sources, etc.) published
- Confidential information open to competent bodies

ACCESSIBILITY
Let the information get to the consumer, not the other way around
- Clearly visible: claim easily found
- Readily accessible: claim close to the product, and at required time and location

ASPIRATIONAL PRINCIPLES

THREE DIMENSIONS OF SUSTAINABILITY
Show the complete picture of product sustainability
- Environmental, social, and economic dimension considered
- Burden shifting between the dimensions avoided
- Complementary certification schemes combined

BEHAVIOUR CHANGE AND LONGER TERM IMPACT
Help move from information to action
- Insights from behavioural science applied
- Consumers actively encouraged to play a role, where appropriate
- Longer-term relationship built with consumer

MULTI-CHANNEL AND INNOVATIVE APPROACH
Engage with consumers in diverse ways
- Various complementing communication channels used
- Different user groups addressed with different channels
- Information complementary and not overloading the consumer

COLLABORATION
Work with others to increase acceptance and credibility
- Broad range of stakeholders included in claim development and communication
- Joint communication channels employed
- Inclusive language used to make consumers feel part of a movement

COMPARABILITY
Help consumers choose between similar products
- Product comparisons substantiated and helpful for consumers
- Approaches initiated by government or third parties followed
- Specific guidance followed

Source: United Nations Environment Programme, International Trade Centre, 2017.

Ten principles of sustainable communication in fashion

Informing, involving and engaging consumers requires firms to respect some key principles of sustainable communication. Given the specific characteristics of the fashion industry, a dedicated decalogue has been created.

In *The Responsible Fashion Company*[16] the ten principles of sustainable communication in fashion are described, as below.[17]

1. *Positive Messages.* Brands should share positive messages in a new story that must be attractive, engaging and credible.
2. *Walk The Talk.* Behaviour should guide communication, not vice versa.
3. *Transparency.* Transparency means having a (single) concept, taking on commitments and objectives and sharing not only the positive outcomes but also the failures.
4. *Accessible, Synthetic and Interactive Information.* Information must be widely available whenever and however people choose. The internet and devices such as smartphones and tablets allow open consultation: content should be developed to be enjoyed and therefore it must be concise and interactive.
5. *Credibility.* Information must be visual, tangible and endorsed by a credible third party, such as an NGO or an authoritative certification body (but beware, there are over 800 certifications worldwide). With or without certification, information must have solid foundations and scientific evidence of what has been done.
6. *Relevance.* Communication should be able to explain why the value of responsibility benefits the consumer.
7. *Storytelling.* The new approach moves from 'what' towards 'how'. it is based on shared values and on explaining how products are made and brought to market.
8. *Courage and Innovation.* Courage and innovation are also necessary when communicating responsibility. Courage could mean rejecting commonplace paradigms, confronting a crisis with great irony or speaking openly about failures.
9. *Simplicity.* It is important to translate numbers and complex concepts into simplified examples that everyone can understand.
10. *Emotion.* Communication is more effective if it triggers emotions or creates mental associations for the audience. Videos are the most efficient tool for simple, direct and engaging storytelling.

---

[16] Rinaldi and Testa, 2014, Chapter 5.
[17] Source: adapted from Rinaldi and Testa, 2014.

2.4 Millennials vs Gen Z: consumer expectations about sustainable fashion

In 2030 the Millennials (Gen Y) and Gen Z will be the two most important generations for fashion purchases.

Millennials are defined as people born from 1980 to 1995; Gen Z are people born from 1995 to 2010.[18]

Millennials are the first generation of digital natives and their affinity for technology helps shape how they shop. They are used to instant access to price comparisons, product information and peer reviews; they are dedicated to wellness, devoting time and money to exercising and eating right. Their active lifestyle influences trends in everything from food and drink to fashion.[19]

Gen Z individuals are true digital natives: from the outset they have been exposed to the internet, to social networks and to mobile systems. That context has produced a hypercognitive generation very comfortable with collecting and cross-referencing many sources of information and with integrating virtual and offline experiences.

Even luxury brands can no longer deny the influence of younger consumers. Millennials and Gen Z accounted for 47% of luxury consumers in 2018 and for 33% of luxury purchases. However, they made up virtually all of the market's growth, compared with 85% in 2017. To capitalize, luxury brands are adapting to the preferences of younger consumers in terms of product offerings, communication and engagement strategies and distribution channels. Younger generations will be the primary engine of growth in the coming years. Generations Y and Z will represent approximately 55% of the 2025 luxury market and will contribute to 130% of market growth between now and then, offsetting a decline in spending by older consumers.[20]

Research confirms that there are some common traits among young generations (i.e. both Millennials and Gen Z) such as:

- the higher interest on sustainability topics compared to previous generations, that makes them seek more information about what is behind the product;[21]

---

[18] Bain&Company – Altagamma Luxury Study, 2017; Goldman Sachs Global Investment Research, 2019.
[19] Goldman Sachs Global Investment Research, 2019.
[20] Bain&Company – Altagamma Luxury Study, 2018.
[21] PwC, 2016; Ipsos-Mori, 2018b.

- willingness to spend a premium price on sustainable products[22] (see Box 5).

Box 5 The interest of young fashion consumers towards sustainability in fashion[23]

During an interview with Erika Andreetta, Partner PwC, Retail & Consumer Goods Consulting Leader, some interesting data came out about the requests of Millennials vs Generation Z in relation to sustainable fashion communication.[24]
The interesting aspect of consumers interested about sustainability is that they are linked together not primarily by demographics, like age or income, but by their values and beliefs. This is not only a cluster of individuals, but also a definition of the market for products and services that these individuals prefer. The market consists of several different segments ranging from organic food to spa and yoga services, to fuel-efficient cars and natural health products and much more.
The current estimate is that consumers interested about sustainability consists of about 100 million people worldwide, approximately 20% of the population in Europe. Global Consumer Insights Survey (GCIS) 2019 research suggests that it could be a good idea for new entrants and longtime industry players to make their story about a green, organic and local lifestyle. Some key data from the PwC global survey:[25]

- 35% of respondents said they choose sustainable products to help protect the environment;
- 37% look for products with environmentally friendly packaging;
- 41% avoid the use of plastic when they can;
- two-thirds of respondents were willing to pay for locally produced food items;
- 42% said they will pay more for sustainably produced non-food items.

Consumers interested about sustainability are demanding, creative, active, well informed and influential. They serve in many markets as early adopters of new consumer behaviour and they tell their friends if they are dissatisfied or enthusiastic with their trials. They are seriously critical about anything that may be labelled as 'fake'. They are the ones who read the small print; look up brands on internet forums and like staying informed through unbiased reviews. They tend to perceive

---

[22] PwC, 2018.

[23] The source for the data mentioned during the interview is the analysis of the trend and impact of multi channels in the 'Made in Italy' sector, through the Total Retail Survey (32 countries, 24,500 consumers) and the Italian insights on Millennials and Generation Z.

[24] PwC Global Consumer Insights Survey (GCIS), 2019, based on a panel of 21,000 consumers in 27 countries (all generations).

[25] PwC Global Consumer Insights Survey (GCIS), 2019, based on a panel of 21,000 consumers in 27 countries (all generations).

brands as authentic when things are done exceptionally well, executed individually and produced by someone demonstrating care.

What holds this group together is their quest for 'The good life with a conscience'. 'Having it all, but not at someone else's expense'. For example, products made by an exploited workforce or from abused animals are rejected.

They search for products that need less transportation and CO_2 emission, use fresh, natural, local ingredients, avoid additives and derive beauty from nature.

Talking about requests of Millennials vs Generation Z in relation to sustainable fashion communication, the 3rd edition of PwC Observatory[26] shows that both generations strongly request fashion companies to communicate more about sustainability and Generation Z values even more sustainable products, compared to Millennials.

Both have inherited a world plagued by issues such as global warming and labour exploitation. Perhaps these are the reasons why they see sustainability as a key factor in their fashion choices? The quality of a product is a fundamental criterion for Millennials and Generation Z when deciding what to buy: 6 people out of 10 ask for quality when they buy clothing and accessories; in addition, 37% prefer to buy sustainable/eco-friendly items; many, if not all, are willing to pay more for environmentally responsible products.

The PwC Observatory report highlights how younger generations are indeed willing to pay a higher price for products with a more responsible impact on the environment and on people's lives: 22% of Generation Z interviewed were willing to pay 5% more for sustainable clothing; 17% of them were willing to pay up to 10% more; the same questions on accessories choices yield similar percentages (21%; 15%).

Millennials are more restrained: 'only' 13% of them would pay 5% more for environmentally sustainable products and 'only' 12% of them are willing to pay up to 10% more.

Source: Interview with Erika Andreetta, Partner, PwC, Retail & Consumer Goods Consulting Leader; PwC Millennials vs Generation Z (2018).

Some issues, though, still need to be resolved:

- the willingness to spend a premium price on sustainable products does not drive towards a real purchase, especially for Gen Z, mainly because of the higher price of sustainable fashion products;

---

[26] 3rd edition of PwC Observatory, 2018, based on a panel of 2,424 Italian consumers, 39% born between 1980 and 1994 (Millennials) and 63% between 1995 and 2010 (Generation Z).

- young consumers (both Millennials and Gen Z) need to be more informed, educated and engaged about sustainable fashion.

For these reasons, fashion companies should start taking more seriously the need of Millennials and Gen Z of knowing their requests for sustainability and start communicating sustainable fashion with a louder voice.

In particular, Gen Z will be likely to contribute to society through technological innovation. By 2030 we can forecast an increased focus on developing products and technologies that will play a role in social action.[27]

Brands that will focus on engagement and one-to-one marketing through technologies (i.e. such as blockchain) will have a key role in interpreting the consumer needs of these younger generations.

References

Bain & Company – Altagamma Luxury Study (2017). Available at: https://www.bain.com/contentassets/0b0b0e19099a448e83af2fb53a5630aa/bain20media20pack_the_millennial_state_of_mind.pdf.

Bain & Company – Altagamma Luxury Study (2018). Available at: https://www.bain.com/contentassets/8df501b9f8d6442eba00040246c6b4f9/bain_digest_luxury_goods_worldwide_market_study_fall_winter_2018.pdf.

BCG–Altagamma (2017). 'The True-Luxury Global Consumer Insight – 4th edition' available on the website https://altagamma.it/media/source/BCG%20Altagamma%20True-Luxury%20Global%20Cons%20Insight%202017%20-%20presentata.pdf.

Ernst & Young (2008). 'LOHAS. Lifestyle of health and sustainability'. Available at https://www.lohas.se/wp-content/uploads/2015/07/ErnstYoung-Studie-2008_ey_LOHAS_e.pdf.

Global Fashion Agenda & BCG. (2017). *The Pulse of the Fashion Industry*. 2017. New York.

Goldman Sachs Global Investment Research (2019). https://www.goldmansachs.com/insights/archive/millennials/.

Ipsos-Mori (2018a). 'Beyond Binary: The lives and choices of Generation Z' available on the website https://www.ipsos.com/sites/default/files/2018-08/ipsos_-_beyond_binary_-_the_lives_and_choices_of_gen_z.pdf.

---

[27] Ipsos-Mori, 2018a.

Ipsos-Mori (2018b). 'Consumer survey report: A baseline survey on EU consumer attitudes to sustainability and supply chain transparency in the fashion industry' available on the website https://www.fashionrevolution.org/wp-content/uploads/2018/11/201118_FashRev_ConsumerSurvey_2018.pdf.

Kreeb, M., Schulz, W., Schwender, C. & Lichtl, M. (2009). 'Das interdisziplinäre Forschungsprojekt balance[f] – Medialisierung der Nachhaltigkeit'. *uwf*, 17, 33. https://doi.org/10.1007/s00550-009-0129-0.

Plummer, J.T. (1974). 'The concept and application of lifestyle segmentation'. *Journal of Marketing*, 1(38), 33–37.

PwC (2016). *Think Sustainability | Summit CNMI* available on the website https://www.pwc.com/it/it/industries/retail-consumer/assets/docs/think-sustainability.pdf.

PwC (2019). *Global Consumer Insights Survey* (GCIS) available on the website https://www.pwc.com/gx/en/consumer-markets/consumer-insights-survey/2019/report.pdf.

PwC (2018). *Millennials vs Generation Z: la sostenibilità cattura i giovani consumatori del fashion*.

Ray, P. & Anderson, R. (2000). *The Cultural Creatives. How 50 Million People Are Changing the World*. New York, Three Rivers Press.

Rinaldi, F.R. & Testa, S. (2014). *The Responsible Fashion Company*. Abingdon, Greenleaf Publishing – Routledge.

Rinaldi, F.R. & Pandolfini, G. (2015). 'Lo Sviluppo della Moda Sostenibile, One size doesn't fit all'*Economia & Management: la rivista della Scuola di Direzione Aziendale dell'Università L. Bocconi*, (6), 36-50.

United Nations Environment Programme (2017). 'Guidelines for providing product sustainability information' available on the website https://www.oneplanetnetwork.org/sites/default/files/guidelines_for_providing_product_sustainability_information_10yfp_ci-scp_2017.pdf.

3 Crafting Innovative Business Models in Fashion

by *Francesca Romana Rinaldi*

> *What we take, how and what we make,
> what we waste, is in fact a question of ethics.*
> Yvon Chouinard

The Value Chain linear model has, since the 1980s, been one of the key models for defining the organization of firms' activities, the fashion industry included. A Renewed Fashion Value Chain model is presented in this chapter to introduce the business models that will be available in the industry by 2030. These models will create partnerships to replace traditional raw materials with sustainable textiles, using recycled materials and chemical-free processes in manufacturing, redesigning the plants and retail points to comply with sustainability principles and commitment to raise people's awareness and the implementation of collaborative consumption platforms to reduce the negative environmental impact of consumer's waste and fashion firms' production leftovers. Innovative business models need to rethink the role of the consumers, who, by 2030, will be much more involved in the value chain than in the past, for example by bringing back the product to the store for recycling or upcycling.

3.1 Innovative business models in fashion

A business model is the way a company is organized – its basic architecture – made up of four interdependent elements: the value proposition, the profit formula, the resources and the key processes.[1]

---

[1] The value proposition is 'an offer system that allows customers to solve a problem more effectively, reliably, practically and conveniently, at a specific price'; the

In order to define a business model in the fashion sector, we need to respond to the following basic questions: what is the value proposition of what is offered to the market? What are the target segments of clientele given the value proposition? Where are the distribution and communication channels to reach the clients and offer them the value proposition? How is the value chain organized? What is the degree of vertical integration?[2]

Once the customer was king – but didn't always have the power that goes with the job title. This is the seismic shift that has occurred: today's customer has that power. Before, the consumer's role on the value chain was limited to the purchase and post-sales phases. Today the consumer not only can but wants to be a part of:[3]

- the company's creative process (R&D, financing), and the marketing and sales activities;
- product customization (innovation and manufacturing);
- the company's entrepreneurial efforts to identify new methods of delivery (distribution).

To satisfy these new expectations, companies will have to open up their value chains and find new ways to involve their customers. This can only be achieved by innovating the 'customer journey' (Figure 4).

---

profit formula is 'the economic model that defines how the company creates value. It specifies the assets and structure of fixed costs, as well as the margins and the speed necessary to cover them'; the key resources are 'the unique nature of the people, technology, products, structures, equipment, financing and trademark, necessary for the value proposition to the customer'; the key processes are 'the means through which a company maintains the value proposition for the customer in a sustainable, repeatable, modular and manageable way' (Johnson, 2010).

[2] Corbellini and Saviolo, 2009.

[3] Accenture/World Economic Forum analysis, 2017.

Figure 4 The integration of the consumer through the value chain

	CROWDFUNDING	OPEN INNOVATION; PERSONALIZATION	CONTENT, COMMUNITY	MAKE AT HOME	SOCIAL COMMERCE	LAST-MILE PARTNERS	CONSUMER INTIMACY CONSUMER AS EMPLOYEE
	R&D FINANCING	INNOVATION	MARKETING	MANUFACTURING	MARKETING AND SALES	DISTRIBUTION	STORE EXECUTION
	BREWDOG	ModCloth	DARBY SMART	SOMABAR	Etsy		
Company Description	Scottish craft beer company	Online retailer of vintage inspired women's clothing!	Online DIY marketplace with innovative ideas and projects that customers can browse, share, shop!	An app controlled robotic bartending appliance used in homes!	Online marketplace for handmade and vintage items!	Logistics company that operates a network of couriers who deliver locally!	An app to help retailers monitor their store operations!
Value Chain Integration	The world's first ever crowdfunded brewery	Identifies community feedback (blog comments, product reviews, social media) as source data for refining its collection	Community connects novice crafters; very active online community	Somabar enables a cocktail to be mixed in seconds from a home kitchen	Enables online users to buys and sell products	Its network of couriers are independent contractors, who could also be customers	App users (real customers who get paid) can assist with store audits (e.g. planogram compliance)

Source: Accenture/World Economic Forum analysis, 2017.

3.2 The active role of consumers[4]

As we have said, innovative business models need to rethink the role of consumers, who have a need to be more active than in the past, for example by bringing back the product to the store for recycling or upcycling. The definition of 'consumer' thus loses its meaning as it assumes the final stage of the transaction as a mere process of purchasing and consuming. It is better to describe the neo-consumer as a 'consum-actor'[5] or 'consum-author',[6] namely a user but, at the same time, an active part of the complex consumption dynamics, increasingly one-to-one, in which the baton passed a long time ago from the brand to the consumer. The new consumption paradigm, as asserted by Fabris, is described by the fact that consumers can be involved in the role of producer-designer-client because they have gained knowledge and awareness from which the company can learn a great deal, translating them into the development of goods and services.

[4] Rinaldi, 2018.
[5] Fabris, 2008.
[6] Morace, 2008.

This new 'customer centricity' in the fashion sector could be implemented in product customization, distribution (omnichannel integration) and communication (transmedia storytelling), through an innovative customer journey (Figure 5).

Figure 5   Towards customer centricity in fashion

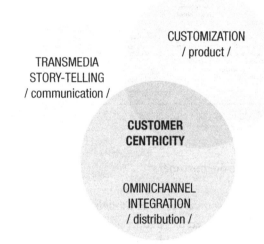

Source: Rinaldi, 2018.

The involvement of the consumer in *product customization* has obvious advantages for the consumer but requires a significant investment by the company in terms of use of personnel and monetary expenditures for the review of the production processes and the timing of the supply chain. This change has a consequence also on the environmental impact: zero-waste, 3D technologies for on-demand production could be used in order to reduce the unsold stocks (see Chapter 9).

The complexity of managing the relationship with the consumer lies also in the fact that the interaction cannot take place only in the store, but through numerous touchpoints (Figure 6).

Figure 6 Customer touchpoints

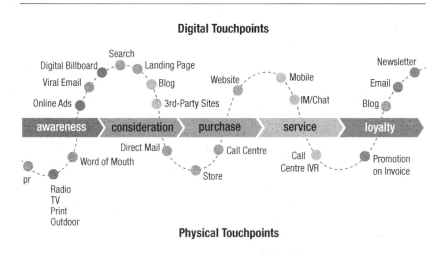

Source: B2Bstories.com, http://b2bstories.com/?attachment_id=38/

For example, in an *integrated omnichannel approach* purchase and delivery options are highly varied. In addition to purchase and direct pick-up in the store by the consumer or purchase through an e-commerce site with home delivery (or preferred address), it is possible to: make purchases in a store with home delivery; make a purchase through an e-commerce site and use the store delivery service; buy online with home delivery from the store or purchase online with a pick-up point or locker delivery service; buy in a store with home delivery if the product is not immediately available; or, lastly, buy in a store with a pick-up point or locker delivery service if the product is not immediately available.[7]

The role of online methods in the contemporary consumer's customer journey can vary depending on whether the internet site is used only to retrieve information, with the customer then preferring to make a purchase in a store (i.e. webrooming), or if it is used to make the actual purchase after having observed and maybe tried the selected products in a physical store (i.e. showrooming).

---

[7] Bettucci *et al.*, 2016.

When a customer-centric approach is applied to communication, the decision is to focus on the consumer and have the message revolve around her, from a *transmedia storytelling* standpoint.

A complete definition of transmedia storytelling is:

> Doing transmedia means to involve multiple media in a publishing project, keeping the features and the language of each one, even if they are part of a single system of integrated communication; it means to make the project's contents available on different technological platforms, without causing any overlaps or interferences, while managing the story experienced by different audiences; it means to allow the multiple media to tell different stories but all exploring a common theme, even if it is experienced through multiple narrative perspectives. Doing transmedia means to agree to give a part of the authorship and responsibility of the tale to the audience and other storytellers in order to create a participatory and synergistic story in the experiences of the different audiences of the tale.[8]

There are various conditions required to ensure that transmedia functions effectively:

- having the possibility to study big data on consumers;
- recognizing the final consumer through the various points of contact with which the message is channelled. We can speak of a 'single customer view';[9]
- guaranteeing consistency between different media, or through the points of contact with the end consumer (Figure 6);
- attempting to establish integration between the various online and offline media.

The new wealth of information offered by big data contributes to improving the quality of the analysis traditionally performed in companies. This is thanks to the use of more integrated and complete data that considers the omnichannel context in which the client moves, and the generation of new profiling criteria which has a greater variety of variables at its disposal. In particular, data that comes from the web has very strong potential.

---

[8] Giovagnoli, 2011.
[9] Bettucci *et al.*, 2016.

The implementation of a well-conceived transmedia storytelling strategy is still rather complicated, time-consuming and costly today, but it is certainly necessary to guarantee the engagement of the Millennial consumer.

3.3 Main drivers of change in fashion: traceability and transparency, circularity, collaborative consumption

The main drivers of change towards the fashion industry 2030 – traceability and transparency, circularity and collaborative consumption – are reshaping the rules of the game determining the success of fashion companies.

The first drivers are traceability and transparency. According to the OECD[10] traceability of value chains enables 'enterprises to track materials and products and the conditions in which they were produced and transformed through the entire value chain'.

According to the European Commission transparency relates directly to relevant information being made available to all elements of the value chain in a standardized way, which allows common understanding, accessibility, clarity and comparison.[11]

A best practice regarding traceability and transparency based on a strong partnership along the fashion and textile pipeline is Candiani Denim. It collaborated with Dondup for the 'D/Zero' collection (Box 6), based on important reductions in the environmental impact of the manufacture of jeans. Another best practice for traceability is Kering in partership with Albini Group, Supima and Oritain (Box 9).

The topic will be discussed in detail in Chapter 4, dedicated to these first drivers.

Box 6 Partnership along the pipeline for responsible fashion: Candiani Denim and Dondup D/Zero collaboration

---

Candiani is a leading company for the production of denim. For over 80 years it has been producing denim for some of the most prestigious names in the market, becoming synonymous with the concepts of 'Made in Italy', 'innovation' and 'sustainability'. All of Candiani's denim is manufactured in Robecchetto con Induno by

---

[10] OECD, 2017.
[11] European Commission, 2017.

means of two factories, where the business activity started in 1938. The company is located in the centre of a natural reserve, Ticino Valley Park, the oldest regional park in Italy, between Milan and the Alps. The layout and the structure of the factory are based on three sustainable principles: reduce, reuse and recycle. In each part of Candiani's production process, there are innovative systems in place that allow the company to run efficiently and with the least amount of water, chemicals and energy possible. The mill is committed to working with sustainable ingredients and developing eco-friendly dyeing and wash technologies. Candiani was the first denim company to use BCI cotton, which today makes up 40% of their overall production. The company also uses organic cotton, hemp, linen and artificial fibres such as TENCEL™ Lyocell with Refibra™ Technology. 100% of Candiani's waste from the spinning, dyeing and weaving process is recycled: 50% is respun into yarn and the other 50% is upcycled into insulation for housing and cars.

As a manufacturer, traceability of raw materials is especially relevant for Candiani Denim. Starting with their most important raw material, cotton, their current approach is to work with two of the most important sustainable cotton programmes – Global Organic Textile Standard and the Better Cotton Initiative. Even if it remains extremely challenging to trace cotton all the way back to the farmer, with these two programmes it is possible to trace the supply back to the ginner, and to be reassured that sustainable farming practices were used and that the farmers were treated well and paid fairly. They also work with a number of alternative fibres that become blended or spun with cotton. Here they also choose to only work with the most sustainable options. These include the already mentioned Lenzing fibres, such as TENCEL™ and Refibra™; custom versions of Roica's recycled elastomer stretch fibre or other fibres from their EcoSmart family; and Q-Nova degradable nylon. Dyes are also an important raw material for Candiani Denim. The company maintains close relationships with its dye suppliers. Many dyes are custom synthesized for Candiani. One example is a dye made by Archroma, which is derived from cotton agricultural waste. Another auxiliary material used in the dyeing process, that was not customized for them but is licensed for use in the denim industry exclusively to Candiani Denim, is Kitotex. Kitotex is a technology created by Canepa SpA, and is made of a polymer Chitosan, which is derived from shrimp shells, a by-product of the food industry and other elements found in nature. While not applicable to every stage in the supply chain, Candiani Denim strives to develop close relationships with the suppliers where the company can also co-collaborate in developing customized or unique products. They find this type of synergy to be a win-win situation for the company, helping Candiani Denim obtain specialized, one-of-a-kind materials, and allowing their suppliers to gain a testing ground for their innovation and ultimately becoming a consistent customer.

The point is, in all of these cases, Candiani Denim knows exactly where the raw materials are coming from and how they are being produced. Candiani Denim tries to keep it all as local as possible, working with suppliers preferably in Italy and, if not, at least those based in Europe.

The company not only prefers to know where their raw materials come from, but also where the final products are going. An example of traceability that is looking downstream is a collaboration with Dondup.

Dondup is a fashion house established in 2000, characterized as having a fresh take on contemporary fashion. Guiding the company's development is a fashion-oriented team composed of the President and shareholder Matteo Marzotto and the CEO Matteo Anchisi, who have transformed Dondup's excellence in Italian-made products into a global company offering both menswear and womenswear and, in its most recent project, childrenswear.

For their D/Zero collection, Candiani Denim helped them make a 100% 'Made in Italy' product. It is a kilometer-zero collection, made with some of Candiani Denim's most sustainable fabrics, constructed in Italy and ultimately washed in Italy using the most sustainable techniques. Excitingly, what was meant to be a capsule collection, will be a mainstay in the Dondup product lineup.

In line with Dondup's motto 'same but different', the D/Zero line comprises six pieces that interpret the iconic staples of the Dondup collections through three main principles:

- D/ZERO is KM0: 100% Made in Italy, born from the collaboration of two leading Italian companies with the same philosophy, operating and producing in Italy;
- D/ZERO is sustainable fabric: raw material crafted by Candiani, recognized for being 'the greenest mill in the blue world';
- D/ZERO is sustainable washes: washes certified according to scientific parameters, with low environmental impact.

Source: corporate material.

The second driver is circularity. The system that dominates industrial production today is defined as 'from the cradle to the grave', a process that follows a linear, unidirectional model: resources are extracted and developed into a product that is sold and ultimately eliminated, buried in a sort of 'grave', usually a mountain of waste or an incinerator. 'Cradle to cradle' projects and certifications aim to create a closed circle, that instead of ending with disposal, considers the discarded product as a nourishing factor that can be reincorporated in a continuous closed cycle without wasting energy or materials.

Best practices for the circularity commitment include Salvatore Ferragamo (see Box 7).

Other examples, such as Stella McCartney, WRÅD and Progetto Quid, will be analysed in Chapter 6, dedicated to this second driver.

Box 7 Salvatore Ferragamo's commitment towards circular fashion

The Salvatore Ferragamo Group, which has always been a byword for top quality and 'Made in Italy' products, is one of the main players in the luxury industry and its origins date back to 1927. The group is mainly active in the creation, production and sale of footwear, leather goods, apparel, silk products and other accessories, as well as fragrances for men and women. In addition, the product range includes eyewear and watches manufactured under licence by third parties in Italy and abroad, with the aim of taking advantage of local traditions and quality.[12]

The promotion of circular economy models and of low environmental impact materials are some of the core pillars of the sustainability strategy of Salvatore Ferragamo.[13]

With the aim of stimulating the level of collaboration and innovation necessary to create a new textiles economy, aligned with the principles of the circular economy, in November 2017 Salvatore Ferragamo signed the 'Manifesto for a Circular Economy', which establishes an alliance to promote innovative and sustainable projects, at Italian level. Moreover, in December 2018, the Salvatore Ferragamo Group took part in the 'Make Fashion Circular' initiative, promoted by the Ellen MacArthur Foundation, established in 2010 with the aim of speeding up the transition towards a circular economy. The brand's participation in the United Nations Global Compact further highlights the commitment towards the virtuous model of circular economy.[14]

The 'Orange Fiber', the 'Rainbow Future' and the '42 Degrees' capsule are among the main projects on circularity implemented in the Salvatore Ferragamo collections. In 2017 the company presented a sustainable capsule collection of womenswear thanks to the collaboration with Orange Fiber, an innovative start-up founded by two young Sicilians, which develops vitaminic textiles from citrus fruit scraps. By reusing the byproduct which the Italian citrus fruit transformation industry produces each year, Orange Fiber has created a sustainable and cosmetic fibre which meets the need for creativity, innovation and eco-sustainability of Salvatore Ferragamo.[15]

In 2018 the company presented to the market 'Rainbow Future', its first shoe inspired by the principles of sustainability. The model transpires from the legendary Rainbow sandal – one of the symbols of Salvatore Ferragamo, made in suede in 1938 for actress Judy Garland – and celebrates the bond between the tradition of 'Made in Italy' and the brand's commitment to sustainable development. Pre-

---

[12] Salvatore Ferragamo Group Sustainability Report, 2018. (https://csr.ferragamo.com/smuseo/images/Custom/pdf-sfogliabile/DNF2018_GruppoFerragamo_eng/docs/DNF2018_GruppoFerragamo_eng.pdf?reload=1553767730196).

[13] Salvatore Ferragamo Group Sustainability Report, 2018.

[14] https://csr.ferragamo.com/en/responsible-passion/circular-economy/.

[15] https://csr.ferragamo.com/en/responsible-passion/orange-fiber/.

sented in a limited edition of 100 pairs in the prestigious Ferragamo's Creations collection, Rainbow Future is a hand-finished platform in veritable wood, crafted in organic crocheted cotton (certified in accordance with the strict environmental and social GOTS – Global Organic Textile Standard criteria), with lining in leather finished with no CO2 emission or water consumption (Layertech technology). Water glue, non-galvanized brass and sewing thread in 100% recycled material complete Rainbow Future, and it comes wrapped in 100% biodegradable cotton bags and 100% recyclable FSC cardboard shoeboxes. Besides this special packaging, each pair of shoes is accompanied by a limited edition certificate, describing its history and special characteristics. Rainbow Future has obtained the ISO 14067 certification, whereby it is possible to calculate the emissions arising from its manufacture and offest them through reforestation programmes, making it a 'carbon neutral' shoe.[16]

In 2019 the company presented the '42 Degrees capsule collection', consisting of a men's sneaker, a women's sneaker, a backpack and a shopping bag, which has been conceived by two young designers from Salvatore Ferragamo – Flavia Corridori and Luciano Dimotta. The capsule collection is the result of an internal competition entered by very young creative talents from Salvatore Ferragamo, according to the brief 'creating accessories with sustainable materials and consistently with the iconic style of the brand'. The result was judged by an international jury of experts, journalists and influencers. All the components of the collection are made of Italian materials and are realized by companies that operate in Italy and have been present on the market for years, combining tradition and innovation and ensuring a transparent and traceable supply chain. The leathers used for bags and shoes have been developed exclusively for Salvatore Ferragamo with wet white chrome and metal-free tanning. The sneaker base is made of calfskin, it is silky to the touch with uniform grain. Soles contain a high percentage of natural rubber, dyed with colours obtained from plants grown on Italian soil. The filler of the cork sole is developed in Sardinia, it is lightweight and adaptable to any shape. The fussbet insole is fully made of organic fibres such as corn, kenaf and wool, and it does not have chemical binders. Linings are water- not solvent-based. The ribbon, the distinctive element of the collection, is made of woven textile, dyed with a system that allows lower levels of consumption of water, fossil fuel and chemicals. It is made with a yarn obtained from an exclusive high-tech polymer, which, thanks to a mechanical and non-chemical process, transforms 100% of plastic bottles, saving water and energy and ensuring lower CO2 emissions compared to conventional polyester. The capsule backpack too has been made with this material. Everything is 100% Made in Italy.[17]

---

[16] https://group.ferragamo.com/it/news/2018/rainbow+future.
[17] Source: corporate material.

The third driver is collaborative consumption. Many companies have applied the logic of the sharing economy to fashion, initiating a phenomenon that has been defined as 'Collaborative Fashion Consumption' (CFC). A formal definition of CFC has been provided by Iran and Schrader,[18] who assert that 'CFC embraces fashion consumption in which consumers, instead of buying new fashion products, have access to already existing garments either through alternative opportunities to acquire individual ownership or through usage options for fashion products owned by others'. Chapter 7 is dedicated to discussing the different business models of CFC: rental, subscription rental and recommerce.

The positive environmental effects of CFC will be discussed together with the limits to the diffusion of the CFC business models. Best practices such as Rent the Runway and Vestiaire Collective (see Box 8, below) will be discussed.

Box 8 Vestiaire Collective as a best practice for luxury recommerce

> According to Bain & Company, the second-hand market is booming, with a growth rate of 9%. It grew from €17 billion in 2015 to €22 billion in 2018 (expected),[19] while some are predicting the industry will almost double by 2023. This is in comparison to a predicted growth rate of 3–5% in the main luxury market.[20]
> The Millennials have largely felt the emergence of recommerce, getting away from the stigma of second-hand fashion, while embracing its lower prices and environmentally conscious supply chain. Vestiaire Collective has grasped this opportunity so the company has to answer to Millennials' needs by investing in technologies which enhance sustainability.
> Vestiaire Collective is a recommerce website for authenticated, pre-owned, luxury fashion products with more than 7.5 million members all over the world who utilize the platform to buy and sell a mix of accessories and clothing.
> Launched in October 2009 in Paris, the company is present in over 50 countries worldwide.[21]

Source: Author's adaptation from www.businessoffashion.com.

---

[18] Iran and Schrader, 2017.
[19] Watches and jewellery are the primary categories in the second-hand market, accounting for 80% of all purchases.
[20] Bain & Company – Altagamma Luxury Study (2018).
[21] www.businessoffashion.com/organisations/vetiaire-collective.

3.4 Responsible innovation: a Renewed Fashion Value Chain model

The concept of Value Chain was introduced for the first time by Michael Porter in his influential 1985 book *Competitive Advantage*.[22]

The Value Chain is a set of activities that an organization carries out to create value for its customers. The way in which activities are performed determines costs and affects the profits: the Value Chain model helped companies' understanding of the sources of value for their organizations. In Porter's Value Chain model, primary and support activities are described. Primary activities (inbound logistics, operations, outbound logistics, marketing and sales, service) relate directly to the physical creation, sale, maintenance and support of a product or service. Meanwhile, support activities (procurement, human resource management, technological development, infrastructure) are so called because support the primary activities for the creation of value. Porter's Value Chain is a linear model refers to the 'cradle to grave' approach. In striving for a 'cradle to cradle' dynamic, a new Value Chain model applied to fashion is needed.

The Renewed Fashion Value Chain model is at the heart of this book. The following chapters will show how the main drivers of change – traceability and transparency, circularity and collaborative consumption – are affecting the value chain activities towards the fashion industry in 2030.

Figure 7 describes the different activities and how the drivers of change affect them.

In the fashion industry in 2030, the supply chain will be fully traceable. The circularity of the value chain will guarantee the sourcing of renewable and sustainable fibres; design and manufacturing will be characterized by circular principles, zero waste, automation, on-demand manufacturing and sales. Packaging will also be circular and logistics will be green.

In 2030 the fashion industry will be much more inclusive and customer-centric. Communication will be based on full transparency. Consumers will receive full care information and guidance on disposal and companies will offer free repairing services.

Consumers will be active thanks to take-back schemes offered by companies. Products will be remanufactured. Consumers will have many options in extending the product lifecycle through buying new products

---

[22] Porter, 1985.

Figure 7 Renewed Fashion Value Chain model

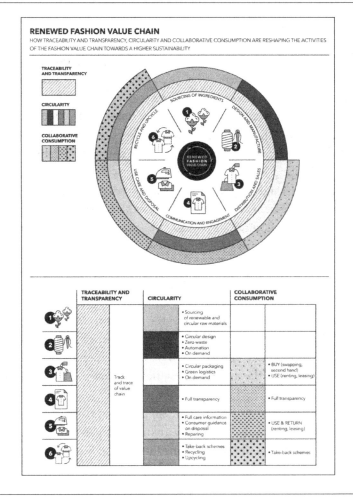

Source: Author's elaboration.

(swapping, second-hand) or through usage options for fashion products owned by others (renting or leasing). Thanks to traceability and transparency, circularity and collaborative consumption, in the 2030 fashion industry the value for each garment will be higher through life extension.

Box 9 examines how responsible innovation is managed by Kering, a leading luxury conglomerate.

Box 9   Responsible innovation at Kering

"Luxury and sustainability are one and the same" is a deeply held conviction of François-Henri Pinault and represents a driver of innovation and value creation for the Kering Group, its Houses, and its stakeholders. A global Luxury group, Kering manages the development of a series of renowned Houses in Fashion, Leather Goods, Jewelry and Watches: Gucci, Saint Laurent, Bottega Veneta, Balenciaga, Alexander McQueen, Brioni, Boucheron, Pomellato, Dodo, Qeelin, Ulysse Nardin, Girard-Perregaux, as well as Kering Eyewear.
Kering sustainability strategy is shaped around three pillars:

- Care, by reducing Kering's environmental footprint and preserving the planet and its natural resources through innovation, new practices, strict standards and original methodologies;
- Collaborate, to bolster stakeholder engagement and promote sustainable luxury. Kering's ambition is to become an exemplary Luxury industry employer, through a safe, stimulating and caring work environment for all its employees;
- Create innovative alternatives, driving change and sharing knowledge.

Some projects can be highlighted in this book.

Worn Again[23]
Worn Again, established in 2005, is a UK based innovation business with a radical vision to eradicate textile waste from the global apparel and textile industry with technology designed as part of a circular resource model. Facing one of the major barrier in textile-to-textile recycling, in 2015 pioneering start-up Worn Again joined forces with H&M and Group Kering to bring to market a revolutionary technology capable of separating blended fibre garments, dyes and other contaminants from polyester and cellulose.

Recycle Material[24]
Gucci was the first luxury brand to use ECONYL® regenerated nylon in ready-to-wear pieces, a 100% recycled nylon fibre derived from fishnets, textile waste and a thick pile fabric used for carpets and upholstery called moquette. Starting in September 2018, Gucci launched a new project, called "ECONYL®-GUCCI PRE CONSUMER FABRIC TAKE BACK PROGRAM" with the aim of recovering any ECO-NYL® regenerated nylon scraps from production and transforms them into a new high-quality yarn.

---

[23] https://www.kering.com/it/news/hm-innovation-company-worn-again-join-forces-make-continual-recycling-textiles-sustainable-reality

[24] http://equilibrium.gucci.com/environment/sustainable-raw-materials/synthetic-fibres/

Clean by Design[25]

Clean by Design – initially developed by the Natural Resource Defense Council (NRDC) – is a programme to improve water and energy efficiency at textile mills. The partnership with Kering, started back in 2014, applied the programme to the luxury industry allowing in three years over 150 energy and water efficiency improvements with an average 2.5 years' return on investment, 100% phase-out of fossil fuels and an average 12% reduction in CO_2 emissions per textile mill. Moreover, the programme resulted in economic savings, closer collaboration and greater transparency.

Traceability innovation driven by forensic science[26]

Traceability is one of the crucial challenges to overcome in fashion's complex global supply chains. Too often indirect sourcing is routine practice and the traditional business model set-up requires many sub-suppliers. This is not always transparent, making it impossible to follow the traceability to, in turn, verify best practices in the supply chain.

A technologically innovative initiative was launched to help solve this issue in cotton's supply chains. As a first in fashion and Luxury, Kering has partnered with Albini Group, Supima and Oritain to create a more sustainable business model through 100% traceable organic cotton. Using forensic science and statistical analysis, the naturally-occurring chemical properties of the actual fibre is analyzed, creating a unique chemical fingerprint that links it back to the field in which it was grown. Subsequently, during every stage of the supply chain, the organic cotton can be verified to ensure the raw material, fabric and final product is consistent with the original fingerprint and has not been substituted, blended or tampered with. Only an exact match shows that the organic cotton is authentic.

Thanks to this procedure, each step is traceable, and it is therefore possible to go back, from the finished fabric, precisely to the field in which the cotton was grown. This pioneering innovation could help Kering come closer to its 2025 goal of 100% traceability in its overall supply chains. Utilizing this platform to understand the provenance of the cotton could enable Kering to implement complete supply chain verification for organic cotton production or the impact it has had on farmers, workers and the environment. This is especially significant where organic cotton is concerned for the Group, since over the last years organic cotton use in the brands' collections has increased, given that Kering's Environmental Profiting and Loss accounting analysis revealed that organic cotton's impact on the environment is 80% less than conventional cotton.

---

[25] https://www.kering.com/it/news/clean-by-design-2017
[26] https://www.kering.com/it/news/kering-launches-a-fashion-first-traceability-innovation-driven-by-forensic-science

> Upon the announcement of the partnership, the Director of Kering's Materials Innovation Lab, Cecilia Takayama, said: "Traceability in fashion's fragmented and global supply chains is imperative to create real change. At Kering we are focused on sustainable raw material sourcing and this innovative technology for our organic cotton supply chain will enable our Materials Innovation Lab greater visibility to verify farming best practices and fibre quality; ensure integrity within the supply chain; and guarantee alignment with our Kering Standards."

Source: https://www.kering.com/en/sustainability/

The next chapters will explore this value creation approach more deeply, and the challenges and opportunities of the Renewed Fashion Value Chain activities will be examined.

3.5 The importance of grassroots innovations for sustainability

Investors are increasingly looking for innovations that have a purpose: with his 2018 letter to CEOs titled 'A Sense of Purpose', Larry Fink, Chairman and Chief Executive Officer of BlackRock had the objective of sharing this exact message.[27]

For this reason too, many fashion and luxury companies and conglomerates are discussing how to integrate 'grassroots innovation' into their processes.

Grassroots innovations are community-led solutions for sustainability. They can offer promising new ideas and practices, but often struggle to scale up and spread beyond small niches.[28]

Grassroots innovations typically involve networks of activists and organizations generating novel bottom-up solutions for sustainable development; solutions that respond to the local situation and the interests and values of the communities involved.[29]

---

[27] Source: https://www.blackrock.com/corporate/investor-relations/2018-larry-fink-ceo-letter.
[28] Source: https://grassrootsinnovations.org.
[29] Hargreaves *et al.*, 2013.

These kinds of bottom-up innovations are guaranteed to stay up to date with the contemporary trends of the industry and consumer needs, but need a high degree of flexibility.

It is generally relatively easy to implement a grassroots innovation in a smaller start-up, whereas it is harder to implement this approach in mainstream fashion and luxury companies and conglomerates. For this reason, some players decide to start working on innovation by building partnerships with start-ups, as in the case of Salvatore Ferragamo and Orange Fiber (see Box 7 and Chapter 6); they create partnerships with incubators or accelerators dedicated to responsible innovation in fashion, as with Kering's support to the Plug & Play innovation accelerator programme at Fashion for Good based in Amsterdam, organizing hackathons for start-ups such as the H-ACK by H-FARM dedicated to the fashion industry or create internal innovation centers.

Patagonia decided instead to create a corporate venture capital fund to support responsible innovation: Patagonia's Tin Shed Ventures (Box 10).

Box 10 Patagonia's 360° sustainability approach and support to responsible innovation to 'save our home planet'

Patagonia grew out of a small company that made tools for climbers. Alpinism remains at the heart of a worldwide business that still makes clothes for climbing—as well as for skiing, snowboarding, surfing, fly fishing, mountain biking and trail running.[30] The company is based in Ventura, California.

Yvon Chouinard, Patagonia founder and owner wrote in "*Let My People Go Surfing*" book the company's philosophy: "We believe the accepted model of capitalism that necessitates endless growth and deserves the blame for the destruction of nature must be displaced. Patagonia and its two thousand employees have the means and the will to prove to the rest of the business world that doing the right thing makes for a good and profitable business."[31]

The company's current mission statement is "We're in business to save our home planet".

> "At Patagonia, we appreciate that all life on earth is under threat of extinction. We aim to use the resources we have—our business, our investments, our voice and our imaginations—to do something about it.

[30] Source: https://www.patagonia.com/company-info.html
[31] Source: https://www.penguin.com/ajax/books/excerpt/9780143109679

As the climate crisis deepens, we see a potential, even probable end to such moments, and so we're fighting to save them. We donate our time, services and at least 1 percent of our sales to help hundreds of grassroots organizations all over the world so that they can remain vigilant, and protect what's irreplaceable. At the same time, we know that we risk saving a tree only to lose the forest—a livable planet. As the loss of biodiversity, arable soils, coral reefs and fresh water all accelerate, we are doing our best to address the causes, and not just symptoms, of global warming.

Staying true to our core values during forty-plus years in business has helped us create a company we're proud to run and work for. To stay in business for at least forty more, we must defend the place we all call home."

Core Values

"Our values reflect those of a business started by a band of climbers and surfers, and the minimalist style they promoted. The approach we take toward product design demonstrates a bias for simplicity and utility."

Build the best product

"Our criteria for the best product rests on function, repairability, and, foremost, durability. Among the most direct ways we can limit ecological impacts is with goods that last for generations or can be recycled so the materials in them remain in use. Making the best product matters for saving the planet."

Cause no unnecessary harm

"We know that our business activity—from lighting stores to dyeing shirts—is part of the problem. We work steadily to change our business practices and share what we've learned. But we recognize that this is not enough. We seek not only to do less harm, but more good."

Use business to protect nature

"The challenges we face as a society require leadership. Once we identify a problem, we act. We embrace risk and act to protect and restore the stability, integrity and beauty of the web of life."

Not bound by convention

"Our success—and much of the fun—lies in developing new ways to do things."[32] In 2013 Patagonia launched Tin Shed Ventures with the objective of investing in start-ups working on responsible innovation:

> "Tin Shed Ventures is Patagonia's corporate venture capital fund, which invests in start-ups that offer solutions to the environmental crisis. Originally launched as $20 Million and Change in May 2013, Tin Shed Ventures partners with businesses focused on building renewable energy infrastructure, practicing regenerative organic agriculture, conserving water, diverting waste and creating sustainable materials. The Tin Shed

---

[32] Source: https://www.patagonia.com/company-info.html

name is rooted in Patagonia's history. In 1957, a young climber named Yvon Chouinard decided to make his own reusable hardware. Using supplies procured from a junkyard, he taught himself how to blacksmith. By 1970, Chouinard Equipment had become the largest supplier of climbing hardware in North America—produced in a tin shed in Ventura, California. But there was a problem. The company's gear was damaging the rock as popular routes had to endure repeated hammering of steel pitons. So Chouinard decided to phase out of the piton business, even though it comprised 70 percent of the company's sales at the time. He introduced an alternative: aluminum chocks that could be wedged in the rock and removed by hand, rather than hammered and left behind. The audacious move worked. Within a few months, the new chocks sold faster than they could be made. Patagonia has since expanded from a climbing hardware company into a global outdoor apparel brand with $800 million in sales while maintaining a strict commitment to sustainability in its products and supply chain. Tin Shed Ventures is funding the next generation of responsible business leaders who share these core values.

We started the fund because we felt existing models for start-up capital were broken. Traditional investors tend to focus on short-term growth and profit, then quickly flip the companies in which they invest. We take a completely different approach to investing. We place environmental and social returns on equal footing with financial returns and provide long-term, patient capital that helps to support forward-thinking entrepreneurs for the long haul. Overall, our aim is to support like-minded start-ups that embody Patagonia's mission statement – We are in business to *save our home planet.*

Because we take this unconventional approach, our coalition of companies has been able to do some incredible things. In addition to investments aiming to reduce greenhouse gas emissions, save water and regenerate soil health, our solar investments are providing clean energy for thousands of households throughout the US. We consistently rally together with fellow B Corps to develop solutions to the environmental crisis and magnify the impact of our investments.

Ultimately, the goal of Tin Shed Ventures is to prove that business—and investments—can be engines for positive change. We're excited to fund and mentor the next generation of responsible businesses, and we hope other investors will join us in doing so."[33]

Sources: www.patagonia.com; http://tinshedventures.com; Chouinard, 2005.

---

[33] Source: http://tinshedventures.com/about/

References

Accenture/World Economic Forum analysis (2017), 'Shaping the Future of Retail for Consumer Industries' available on the website http://www3.weforum.org/docs/IP/2016/CO/WEF_AM17_FutureofRetailInsightReport.pdf.

Bain & Company – Altagamma Luxury Study (2018). Available at: https://www.bain.com/contentassets/8df501b9f8d6442eba00040246c6b4f9/bain_digest__luxury_goods_worldwide_market_study_fall_winter_2018.pdf.

Bettucci, M., D'Amato, I., Perego, A. & Pozzoli, E. (2016). *Omnicanalità*, Milan, Egea.

Chouinard, Y. (2005). *Let my People Go Surfing: The Education of a Reluctant Businessman*. New York, Penguin Press.

Chouinard, Y. (2016). *Let My People Go Surfing: The Education of a Reluctant Businessman – Including 10 More Years of Business Unusual*. New York, Penguin Press.

Corbellini, E. & Saviolo, S. (2009). *Managing Fashion and Luxury Companies*. Milan, ETAS.

Decker, V. (2016). 'Fanny Moizant's Vestiaire Collective is a major player in the luxury consignment market', Forbes. Available at: www.forbes.com/sites/viviennedecker/2016/12/26/fanny-moizants-vestiaire-collective-is-a-major-player-in-the-luxury-consignment-market/#76482b8d35f6/.

European Commission (2017). 'A Background Analysis on Transparency and Traceability in the Garment Value Chain', Final Report (September).

Fabris, G. (2008). *Societing*. Milan, Egea.

Galbiati, L. (2019). 'Vestiaire Collective: finanziamento da 40 milioni di euro a supporto di crescita e tecnologia', Fashion Network. Available at: https://it.fashionnetwork.com/news/Vestiaire-Collective-finanziamento-da-40-milioni-di-euro-a-supporto-di-crescita-e-tecnologia,1111633.html#.XR0SougzbIU.

Giovagnoli, M. (2011). *Transmedia Storytelling: Imagery, Shapes and Techniques*. Halifax, ETC Press.

Hargreaves, T., Hielscher, S., Seyfang, G. & Smith, A. (2013). 'Grassroots innovations in community energy: The role of intermediaries in niche development', *Global Environmental Change*, 23(5) (October), 868–880.

Iran, S. & Schrader, U. (2017). 'Collaborative fashion consumption and its environmental effects', *Journal of Fashion Marketing and Management: An International Journal*, 21(4), 468–482.

Johnson, M. W. (2010). *Seizing the White Space: Business Model Innovation for Growth and Renewal*. Boston, Harvard Business Press.

Lunghi, C., Rinaldi, F.R. & Turinetto, M. (eds.) (2018). *What's Fashion? It's Method!* Milan, BUP.

McDonough, W. & Braungart, M. (2002). *Cradle to Cradle: Remaking the Way We Make Things*. New York, North Point Press.

Morace, F. (2008). *Consum-autori. Le generazioni come imprese creative*. Milan: Scheiwiller.

OECD (2017). 'Due Diligence Guidance for Responsible Supply Chains in the Garment and Footwear Sector' available on the website https://mneguidelines.oecd.org/OECD-Due-Diligence-Guidance-Garment-Footwear.pdf.

Padula, G. & Rubera, G. (2015). 'Selfie, big data e customer intelligence', *Economia & Management*, 1 (January–February), 19-22.

Porter, M.E. (1985). *Competitive Advantage*. New York, The Free Press.

Rinaldi, F.R. (2018). 'Fashion future: Crafting innovative business models in fashion', in Lunghi, C., Rinaldi, F. R. & Turinetto, M. (eds.), *'What's Fashion? It's Method!'*. Milan, BUP, chapter 3.

Rinaldi, F.R. & Pandolfini, G. (2015). 'Lo Sviluppo della Moda Sostenibile, One size doesn't fit all'*Economia & Management (6)*, 36-50.

Rinaldi, F.R. & Testa, S. (2014). *The Responsible Fashion Company*. Abingdon, Greenleaf Publishing – Routledge.

Salvatore Ferragamo Group Sustainability Report (2018). Available at: https://csr.ferragamo.com/smuseo/images/Custom/pdf-sfogliabile/DNF2018_Gruppo-Ferragamo_eng/docs/DNF2018_GruppoFerragamo_eng.pdf?reload=1553767730196.

4 Enhancing Transparency and Traceability for Sustainable Value Chains in the Garment and Footwear Industry

by *Maria Teresa Pisani*[1]

> *You must do the things you think you cannot do.*
>
> Eleanor Rooslvelt

The garment and footwear (GF) industry has one of the biggest environmental footprints and poses great risks for human health and society. At the same time, the complexity and opacity of the value chain makes it difficult to identify where such impacts occur and to devise necessary targeted actions. In the next decades, fast fashion trends, coupled with growing demand in emerging economies, are going to intensify the effects on the environment and human health of practices and processes, and on working conditions. Key actors in the industry have identified interoperable and scalable traceability and transparency of the value chain, as crucial enablers of more responsible consumption and production patterns, in line with SDG 12, of the United Nations Agenda for Sustainable Development.[2]

---

[1] The views expressed herein are those of the author and do not necessarily reflect the views of the United Nations.

[2] This chapter is a summary of the study conducted in connection with the United Nations sabbatical programme undertaken by Maria Teresa Pisani, for the Economic Cooperation and Trade Division of UNECE, during the period May–October 2018. The findings have been presented at the OECD Due Diligence Forum for the Garment and Footwear Sector in February 2019, and submitted to the 25th Plenary of the United Nations Centre for Trade Facilitation and e-Business, in April 2019.

For their contribution to this study, I thank Prof. Guido Giuseppe Corbetta and Francesca Romana Rinaldi of the Bocconi University; Frans Van Diepen of the Ministry of Economy of the Netherlands; Gustavo Gonzalez-Quijano, COTANCE Euroleather; Sabrina Frontini, ICEC; Benedetta Francesconi of the Ministry of Economic Development of Italy; Olga Pirazzi of Cittadellarte Fashion Best; Digna Wer-

4.1 A globalized industry with an enormous environmental footprint and societal risks

The clothing market was valued at US$3 trillion in 2017 and represents 2% of the world GDP,[3] and is expected to accelerate its pace, with an annual growth rate estimated at 2.1% between 2017 and 2022[4]. Globally, the industry employs more than 60 million workers[5], with most of them in the upstream part of the value chain and in less developed countries (LDCs), and up to 75% of these workers being women[6]. Currently, clothing represents about 5% of total manufactured goods exported in the world[7], with China leading (36%), followed by the EU (28%), Bangladesh (6.4%), Vietnam (5.5%) and India (4%).

In 2018, the sector appears to have reached a tipping point, with more than half of the sales of garments and footwear going to emerging markets located in Asia-Pacific, Latin America and other regions, as more people in such regions have joined the middle class. This evolution lies in the phasing out of the Multi-Fibre Arrangement (MFA) that had governed the world trade of clothing from 1994 to 2004 through quotas on developing countries' exports to advanced economies[8]. Coupled with the accelerated adoption of disruptive technology, digitalization across the value chain, adoption of innovative business models and proliferation of data, this has led to the globalization and fragmentation of the industry value chain, and a move towards faster and more flexible production models[9].

The increasing delocalization trend of the upstream part of the supply chain has been certainly due to the opportunity to benefit from cheaper labour costs and less stringent and demanding legislation on labour rights in developing economies. It is reported in fact that nine out of ten women and girls employed in the industry in emerging economies, earn less than

---

ster, Charles Frei and Thomas Malik of the United Nations Economic Commission for Europe; Mauro Chezzi of Confindustria Moda.

[3] Market size estimates based on triangulation of Euromonitor International (Apparel and Footwear) 2017, Fashion United (2015), Boston Consulting Group (2017).
[4] Euromonitor, 2017.
[5] Fashion United, 2018.
[6] ILO, 2017.
[7] WTO, 2017.
[8] European Commission, 2017.
[9] McKinsey & Company, 2018.

a living wage[10]. Consumers have responded to lower prices and a greater variety by buying more items of clothing. In fact, the number of clothing items produced each year has doubled since 2000 and exceeded 100 billion in 2014.[11]

As a result, the environmental footprint has increased dramatically, mainly happening in raw material production and manufacturing in developing countries. Indeed, while natural fibre cultivation involving pesticides results in decreased soil fertility and water pollution, in the manufacturing stage the industry has an environmental footprint mainly linked to discharge of pollutants and water consumption (79 million m^3/year of water consumption), and it is no secret that the clothing sector consumes very high levels of energy and plays a role in climate change (1,715 million tons/year CO_2 emissions).[12] When it comes to the health risks associated with the handling of chemicals, and the illnesses that are a by-product of using such substances, it is reported that 10% of textile-related substances are of potential concern to human health, and that 8% of dermatological diseases are due to the clothing we wear.[13]

Such risks and impacts are expected to grow further, following an increase in global fashion consumption by 63% (from 62 to 102 million tons) between 2015 and 2030. It is also a result of fast fashion trends, that has led to an average increase from two to about five fashion cycles a year. This has put great emphasis on the need to investigate waste production and the issues of reuse and recyclability, starting from the fibre stage of the supply chain, and looking towards a circularity approach.

4.2 Transparency and traceability as a means to enhance sustainability of a complex and opaque value chain

Important ingredients to mitigate sustainability risks and impacts in the sector, include: 1) improving working conditions of employees in the raw material production and manufacturing stages, especially in the upstream segments of the value chain; 2) improving the environmental footprint

---

[10] ILO, 2017.
[11] McKinsey & Company, 2018.
[12] Strähle et al., 2015.
[13] Associazione Tessile e Salute, 2014.

of products and production processes throughout the entire value chain, including aspects such as use, reuse and recycling, in line with a circular economy approach; 3) moving consumers' attitudes towards more intelligent and ethical consumption; 4) ensuring that final consumers receive accurate and relevant information about the social, environmental and health risks of what they buy.[14]

The complexity and opacity of the value chain makes it difficult to identify where impacts occur and to devise necessary targeted actions. Key actors in the industry have identified interoperable and scalable traceability and transparency of the value chain, as crucial enablers of more responsible consumption and production patterns, in line with SDG 12, of the United Nations Agenda for Sustainable Development, with target 12.6 inviting Member States to encourage companies to adopt and report on sustainability practices, and target 12.8, which relates to ensuring that people everywhere have the relevant information and awareness for sustainable development and lifestyles.

Before entering into the core of the chapter, few definitions are needed.

- *Traceability* is understood as 'the ability to trace the history, application or location of an object' in a supply chain.[15] In this context, it is defined as the ability to identify and trace the history, distribution, location and application of products, parts and materials, to ensure the reliability of sustainability claims, in the areas of human rights, labour (including health and safety), the environment and anti-corruption;[16] and 'the process by which enterprises track materials and products and the conditions in which they were produced through the supply chain'.[17]
- *Transparency* relates directly to relevant information been made available to all elements of the value chain in a standardized way, which allows common understanding, accessibility, clarity and comparison.[18]
- *Sustainability*, in this context, is understood as the manufacturing, marketing and use of garment, footwear and accessories, and

---

[14] European Commission, 2017.
[15] ISO, 2015.
[16] Norton *et al.*, 2014.
[17] OECD, 2017.
[18] European Commission, 2017.

its parts and components, taking into account the environmental, health, human rights and socio-economic impacts, and their continuous improvement through all stages of the product's life cycle (design, raw material production, manufacturing, transport, storage, marketing and final sale, to use, reuse, repair, remake and recycling of parts and components).[19]

This chapter explores how the traceability and transparency of value chains can help advance the sustainability of the garment and footwear sector. It highlights that transparency and traceability must be a collaborative effort, investigates requirements for and components of robust new schemes and provides a series of recommendations on possible measures for public authorities. In particular, it addresses the following research questions:

1. How can transparency and traceability of the value chains help advance sustainability of the GF sector?
2. What are the key requirements for the business sector to put in place a robust transparency and traceability scheme?
3. What possible measures could public authorities (national/regional/international) devise to support traceability and transparency of sustainable GF value chains?

To answer these questions, quantitative and qualitative analyses have been conducted through targeted interviews and field visits, and the collection of input through a survey questionnaire, engaging more than 100 companies from all over the world, from the textile (68%), and the leather sector (21%), and those covering both sectors (11%). In terms of geographical representation, more than 80% of the 100 companies that took part in the survey are from the European Union, while the rest are from the USA, from Africa (1 from South Africa) and from Asia, with the rest having provided anonymous responses.

---

[19] UNECE, 2018.

4.3 Companies' strategies for sustainable production patterns

Due to growing concerns about the industry's footprint, sustainability practices are receiving increased attention. Consumers are getting more and more concerned about the ethical and environmental impacts of their purchases. In 2015, a survey in 60 countries found that 66% of consumers are ready to pay more for products or services from companies committed to sustainability.[20] And more recent studies show that conscious consumers increasingly live in emerging economies, are educated, with high income and children below the age of 17.[21] At the same time, challenges for the sector have intensified and new drivers have emerged – such as product safety, product authentication (anti-counterfeit), sustainability and corporate social responsibility (CSR).[22]

Companies are therefore starting to think not only in terms of economic profit but also of sustainability and of the societal values they create, in order to manage reputational risks. In fact, most of the companies surveyed have a formal sustainability strategy in place, especially focused on their internal operations and own facilities, at the level of raw material extraction and production in the manufacturing and assembling process, or at the design stage. However, when it comes to addressing sustainability risks and impacts along the value chain and requesting compliance with environmental and social standards to suppliers and subcontractors, the level is lower (less than 40%).

Regarding environmental risks, sustainability approaches mainly investigate levels of energy and water consumption, use of chemicals, production waste treatment and recycling and CO2 emissions in production processes. Increasing attention is also paid to circular approaches in terms of reuse, recycling and green R&D. However, there is less attention to impacts in the upstream part of the value chain, such as the environmental footprint of raw material production. When it comes to working towards compliance with sustainability claims, 51% of surveyed companies mentioned they have voluntary certification/s on sustainability performances (see Figure 8).[23]

---

[20] Nielsen, 2015.
[21] Euromonitor International, 2018.
[22] GS1, 2018.
[23] For raw materials: GOTS, FSC, GRS, OEKO TEX, Associazione Tessile e Sa-

Figure 8   Environmental and Social/Ethical Risks in Sustainability Approaches

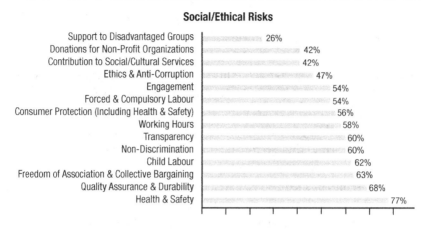

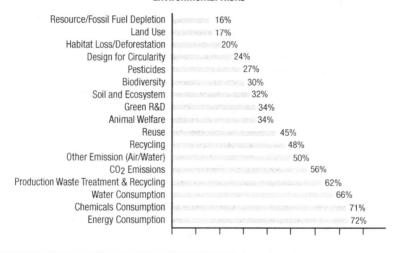

Source: UNECE, 2017 & UN/CEFACT Plenary, April 2019.

It is also worth mentioning that companies are becoming increasingly aware of the relevance of their sustainability approaches to achieving the SDGs (38% of respondents).

---

lute are the most mentioned; for products: OEKO TEX, GOTS, USI 140001-S001-18001, Associazione Tessile e Salute, Serico, FSC, Detox are the most mentioned; for internal production: ISO 14001, OEKO TEX, Standard 100, GOTS, INDITEX, Associazione Tessile e Salute, FSC, Detox are the most mentioned.

4.4 Meeting an ever-increasing demand for trusted information

Brands, retailers, suppliers, processors, manufacturers, distributors, logistics providers and solution providers, regulators – and indeed consumers – are all demanding fast, accurate and complete information that can be seamlessly accessed across traceability systems.[24] However, it is a challenge for companies to meet the ever-increasing demand for trusted information about the products consumers purchase and wear or use without a framework to ensure that traceability systems are interoperable and scalable.

Products within this sector are the result of numerous production phases, and the interaction of multiple economic actors that exchange raw materials, semi-finished goods, parts, components and finished goods. In addition, there are large geographical and cultural distances between retailers and brands on the one hand and farmers and manufacturers on the other. Therefore, sustainability can't be achieved within the boundaries of a company's own operations but must be pursued and traced throughout the entire value chain.[25]

Improving traceability and transparency are key means to investigate and collect most of the data needed to qualitatively and quantitatively assess the environmental and social sustainability of a value chain, and as the first necessary step in the roadmap for scaling up sustainable patterns.[26] Traceability is the capacity to substantiate a claim via the collection of relevant data generated along the value chain (history, distribution, location and application of products, parts and materials). Its application allows the mapping of the business and production flows, from farming and raw materials extraction to semi-finished product and parts production to final product manufacturing, retail and possibly use and reuse, in line with a circular economy approach[27]. This requires the active collaboration of partners involved in the same production network. By using this approach, each actor can include in its network the sustainable partners, which can adopt the same method for the selection of their own suppliers. The next step is transparency, which relates directly to relevant information being made available to all parties and actors of the value chain in a standard-

---

[24] GS1, 2018.
[25] Winter and Lash, 2016; OECD, 2017.
[26] BCG and GFA, 2018.
[27] Agrawal et al., 2016.

ized way, which allows common understanding, accessibility, clarity and comparison.[28]

> 'How can transparency and traceability of the value chains help advance sustainability in the garment and footwear sector?' This is the first research question addressed in this chapter. In fact, key actors in the industry have identified traceability and transparency as crucial enablers for change towards more responsible production and consumption patterns, and as the first core priority for immediate implementation[29]. It allows connection between producers and firms, as well as firms, brands and retailers, and provides a rigorous way of collecting information related to operations and products along the value chain. Table 3 reports the results of the survey conducted for this study, which highlights the business sector views on the key benefits of traceability in garment and footwear value chains.

According to respondents, traceability helps companies to build trust with consumers, along with stronger relationships and more solid networks with clients and suppliers. It also helps identify opportunities for efficient and sustainable management of resources, as well as risks for health, the environment and labour rights. Presenting the information in a standardized form supports common understanding, accessibility, clarity and comparison, and fosters credible communication towards consumers and the public.

To address this research question, the study has investigated research papers and has conducted face-to-face interviews with multi-stakeholders. They highlight that traceability and transparency of the value chain are important preconditions for sustainability and are key for identifying and monitoring risks and impacts, sustaining the reliability of claims and companies' accountability, reducing public pressures and for making relevant information available to final consumers.

The ITC Sustainability Map (Box 11) is a best practice, being the first IT platform in the garment and footwear sector for the exchange of social and labour audits against a common framework.

---

[28] European Commission, 2017.
[29] CEO Agenda, 2018; BCG and GFA, 2018.

Table 3   The benefits of traceability

Consumers' trust	More accurate information to consumers regarding product safety, due to availability of more robust and complete product data used in B2B and B2C processes. This is to be coupled to more accurate and rapid detection and deterrence of counterfeit products
Reputational risk management	More efficient and accurate sustainability and CSR information, resulting from increased transparency and automated recording and sharing of traceability data. This allows companies to better address pressures from civil society, media, politicians and regulators, regarding products and operations claims
Efficient supply chain/ resource management	Cost savings resulting from simplified and automated business processes such as inventory management, but also from better information and control over resource use (water, energy, chemicals, etc.)
Enhanced communication with business partners	More accurate and complete information exchange helps improve communication with business partners along the value chain

Source: UNECE, 2017 and UN/CEFACT Plenary, April 2019; GS1, 2018; Kumar *et al.*, 2017.

Box 11   The ITC Sustainability Map

> To complement the work of the UNECE-UN/CEFACT to establish a global Traceability Standard for sustainable value chains in the garment and footwear sector, the International Trade Centre (ITC) is working to the development of an online Sustainability Map Platform. This is a freely accessible database – a global public good – that stores sustainability standards and enables companies to understand where its code of conduct stands, opening up sourcing opportunities and creating a level playing field in regard to social and environmental criteria.
>
> The ITC's project underway in partnership UNECE, and with support of the European Commission, is about making the sector more accountable and transparent. A great deal of fashion players, representing more than 40% of the fashion industry, have gathered to agree upon an IT base for the exchange of social and labour audits against a common framework. Concretely, they will put their code of conducts into the ITC platform so that it can be used and shared by suppliers/ providers worldwide.
>
> This practice will drive down the audit cost for brands and manufacturers. The challenge here is to make brands, including fast fashion brands, switch from competing on sustainability to competing on the product, while agreeing on a minimum common set of social and labour criteria. The UN Traceability Standard and the Sustainability Map Platform are expected to be completed by 2021.

Source: ITC.

4.5 Challenges and opportunities to achieving value chain traceability and transparency

Tracking and tracing the value chain is a challenging task because of the organizational and technological complexities for the industry.[30] This is confirmed by the survey, whose results indeed point out that only 34% of companies have a traceability approach in place, of which half has visibility up to Tier 2 (material manufacturing or finished materials production) only (see Figure 9).

Figure 9 Traceability of the value chain in the garment and footwear sector

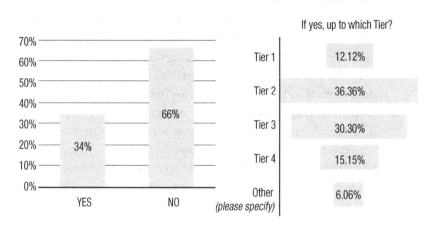

Note: In the right-hand graph, 'Other' refers to chemical suppliers.

Source: UNECE 2017 and UN/CEFACT Plenary, April 2019.

In the survey, respondents view key challenges as mainly in relation to:

1. The *fragmentation and complexity of the business network* (for 69% of respondents) often makes it difficult for companies to track products' history and features. Multiple actors with different systems and requirements contribute to production across international borders, and some areas in a supply chain are especially opaque.

---

[30] Kumar *et al.*, 2017.

However, technological advances (e.g. blockchain, bar codes, chips) may make this increasingly more manageable;
2. *Privacy of data and data security* (for 55% of respondents), which are of concern particularly for brands, traders and companies in the high-value segment of the market, as they are often ready to share information about specialized providers.
3. The *costs associated with the necessary resources and technologies* for the implementation of such schemes, also due to increasing amounts of data and information to manage and inventory volumes (for 49% of respondents). Traceability requires substantial investment in technology and processes aimed at performing various levels of verification on products, parts and components at all stages of the value chain.
4. *Technological barriers.* Indeed, technological advances such as blockchain and distributed ledger technologies, bar codes and chips, offer an opportunity. Mastering these technologies is a challenge, also due to regulatory uncertainty and perceived legal risks, data protection laws that vary across geographies, and interoperability between existing evolving platforms and lack of standards. These costs are a concern for many actors pursuing traceability, which is the case especially for non-vertically integrated companies or brands and SMEs (29% of respondents). When leadership is there, and collaboration is widespread, there is an incentive for actors to work together, which lowers costs overall.

When it comes to transparency and the disclosure of information about suppliers, location of production sites and compliance with sustainability standards in companies own operations and suppliers, only 28% of companies make their suppliers list publicly available. The same share of companies produces a sustainability report that covers the environmental/social and ethical risks and impacts. Such reports are mainly addressed to the public, the clients'/suppliers' base and investors, and are disclosed though companies' websites. But having or disclosing information about Tier 1/Tier 2 suppliers is not enough. Traceability is required through the whole value chain. According to the 'Pulse of the Fashion Industry' 2018 report, two-thirds of negative sustainability impact occurs at the raw materials stage (Tier 4).

The second research question discussed in this chapter is 'What are the key requirements for the business sector to put in place a robust transparency and traceability scheme?'. According to the survey's respondents, key data/information to be exchanged through a robust traceability system for sustainable value chain in the sector should include information on the country of origin of the main products, parts and components of garment and footwear (81% of respondents), features and properties of raw material and products (78% of respondents), information on the processing steps (58% of respondents) and compliance with sustainability requirements in terms of social, environmental and health risks and impacts (56% of respondents). Other types of data should relate to costs, responsible parties, transport modalities and trade transactions.

When it comes to technical standards to exchange such information and data, the GS1 Global Standards provides general guidelines to identify, capture and share supply chain data. They define business process and system requirements for full supply chain traceability, although the standards developed so far do not focus specifically on textile and leather value chains. The EU Ecolabel, the Global Organic Textiles Standard (GOTS) and the Fairtrade Textiles Standards all contain elements of traceability implementation for textiles. All together, these standards and guidelines do not cover all the materials and types of production used in textile and leather value chains, thus do not encompass every single stage of the value chain. This makes it hard for companies and consumers to navigate and to choose which model to use. Based on such indications, a cornerstone of a traceability framework would be a standardized representation of business processes, business transactions and information entities (*Business Requirement Specifications BRS*), to map and describe the exchange of data for the traceability of raw materials, products, parts and components, during extraction, processing, assembling, transport, within a country or across borders, as well as location and responsible parties. Such a scheme should also map and describe the exchange of data related to the origin of raw materials, textile products, parts and components, and how they have been made, including with respect to social, environmental and health requirements, based for instance, on a complete set of sustainability criteria, like those included in the OECD Due Diligence Guidelines for Multinational Enterprises. This will allow the exchange of certificates for compliance sustainability requirements.

The framework should also provide for the standardization of the basic structure of supporting business documents (*Core Component Business Document Assembly CCBDA*) and describe the information exchanged in a business interaction in textile and leather value chains, in a syntax and technology neutral way. In addition, an *XML and/or EDIFACT message scheme* should provide for the harmonized electronic exchange of data and certificates B2G and B2B that supports the business processes for sustainable value chains. Finally, implementation guidelines should be made available for usage of the message and exchange mechanisms, including the specification of identifiers for product, parties and locations and other devices, and use of code lists.[31]

4.6 Policy and legislation in support of transparency and traceability of value chains

The third research question discussed in this chapter is: 'What are possible measures that public authorities (national/regional/international) could devise to support traceability and transparency of sustainable GF value chains?'.

The results of this study highlight the relevance of policy as a key driver for advancing transparency and traceability of value chains. Compliance with national, regional or international regulatory requirements or guidance directives and common criteria to measure and benchmark sustainability performance, coupled with an effective auditing system for compliance and alert on violations, is a priority for companies (75% of respondents), which have also stressed the need for fiscal incentives (64%) and support to R&D (54%) and training for skills development (61%).

For the GF sector, at the regional level, Regulation (EC 907/2006) of the European Parliament and of the Council REACH mandates the traceability for all chemical substances, including those used in garments and footwear manufactured in or imported into Europe. Also, in 2011, the EU adopted a Regulation (EU 1007/2011) on textile names and the related labelling of textile products, while in April 2014, the European Parliament voted that manufacturers should be required to label all non-food goods with their country of origin. Finally, an EU Regulation (1007/2011) concerns the marking and labelling of the composition of products fibres and other information for the consumer on products quality.

---

[31] UN/CEFACT, 2015.

At the international level, the OECD Due Diligence Guidance for Responsible Supply Chains in the GF Sector encourages enterprises to take a due diligence approach and implement traceability and transparency systems. The guidelines stress the need to collect and record information regarding companies' ownership structure, location, size and nature of production stage, suppliers and intermediaries operating at Tier 1 (suppliers and intermediaries/trading agents). They also emphasize the importance of working towards mapping all suppliers of Tier 2, and account for progress over time, with the supply chain mapping including information on subcontractors, as far as possible. Companies should also work towards identifying the country of origin for all materials or components sourced from high-risk areas.

The UN Global Compact also provides guidance to help companies and stakeholders understand and advance supply chain traceability and provides practical steps for implementing traceability programmes within companies. The UN Guiding Principles on Business and Human Rights impose obligations for corporations to practice due diligence covering 'adverse human rights impact that the business enterprise may cause or contribute to through its own activities, or which may be directly linked to its operations.

A targeted policy document should be therefore developed providing vision and objectives for a global transparency and traceability system. Such a policy should also explore the potential application of new technologies, for example, blockchain and other distributed ledger technologies, IoT, AI and the use of electronic identifiers and labels.

4.7 Conclusions and recommendations

Traceability and transparency are crucial enablers for responsible production and consumption patterns. Traceability helps companies to build trust with consumers, along with stronger relationships and more solid networks with clients and suppliers. It also helps identify opportunities for efficient and sustainable management of resources, as well as risks for health, the environment and labour rights. However, the numerous existing standards and guidelines do not cover all the materials and types of production used in the sector, and do not encompass every single stage of the value chain.

A Sectoral Framework for Traceability and Transparency of the Value Chain, that is interoperable and scalable, could be the solution. It would allow an effective connection between producers and firms, as well as firms, brands and retailers. The recommendations regarding the main elements of such a sectoral framework are as follows:

Recommendation 1: To develop a comprehensive *Technical Global Standard for the Traceability of Sustainable Value Chains in the Garment and Footwear Sector*, covering the entire lifecycle of products, consisting of:

- *Component 1*: A standardized representation of business processes, business transactions and information entities (*Business Requirement Specifications BRS*), to map and describe the entire value chain in the GF sectors, including sustainability risks at key nodes of the production and consumption process.
- *Component 2*: A standardized basic structure of supporting business documents (*Core Component Business Document Assembly CCBDA*) and a description of the information exchanged in a business interaction in textile and leather value chains, in a syntax- and technology-neutral way.
- *Component 3*: An *XML and/or EDIFACT message schema* to provide for the harmonized electronic exchange of data and certificates B2G and B2B that supports the business processes for sustainable value chains in the textile and leather sector.
- *Component 4*: Finally, *implementation guidelines* should be made available for usage of the message and exchange mechanisms, including the specification of identifiers for product, parties and locations and other devices, and use of code lists.[32]

A Transparency and Traceability Framework also needs a targeted *Policy/Regulatory Framework*, providing its objectives along with implementation phases, a distribution model of costs and benefits among stakeholders, rules for collaboration, a framework for data exchange, including sustainability risks, rules on confidentiality and measurement of performance. It should also explore the application of supporting new technologies (e.g. blockchain and other distributed ledger technologies).

---

[32] UN/CEFACT, 2015.

Recommendation 2: To develop a *Policy/Regulatory Framework*, enabling governments to advance the necessary policy and regulatory approaches and to support parties along the value chain in their efforts to implement improvement plans, assess themselves against recognized international initiatives, standards, codes of conduct and audit protocols.

- *Principle 1*: It should be based on a holistic, multi-stakeholder approach, aiming to ensure traceability for the whole lifecycle and value chain of a product, with its parts and components, and requiring companies to cover the entire set of sustainability criteria (e.g. the requirements of the OECD Due Diligence Guidelines).
- *Principle 2*: It should include a standardized set of criteria for reporting on the sustainability performance of different parties of the value chain and encourage transparency.
- *Principle 3*: It should provide a roadmap for continuous improvement and set the bar high enough to only acknowledge companies that go above and beyond average performance and which are committed to continuous improvement.
- *Principle 4*: It should also be science-based and reflect regulatory improvements.

The framework, that is, the *Technical Standard and the Policy Recommendation*, could be developed by the United Nations Centre for Trade Facilitation and e-Business UN/CEFACT considering its mandate and expertise on traceability schemes for sustainable value chains, through a multi-stakeholder consultation approach. This would provide a global and neutral platform, for the development of the supporting normative framework to help the industry achieving the relevant SDGs of the 2030 Agenda for Sustainable Development.

References

Alves *et al.* (2014). 'Fairtrade: Applying semantic web tools and techniques to the textile traceability'.
Associazione Tessile e Salute (2016). 'Linee Guida sui requisiti eco-tossicologici per gli articoli di abbigliamento, pelletteria, calzature ed accessori'.
Business Wire – A Berkshire Hathaway Company. 'Global Leather Goods Market (2016–2022) – By Mode of Sale, Product & Region – Research and Market'.

Available at: https://www.businesswire.com/news/home/20170920005683/ en/ Global-Leather-Goods-Market-2016-2022---Mode (accessed 19 September 2018).

Changing Market Foundation (2018). 'The false promise of certification'.

Clean Clothes Campaign (2017).'Follow the thread: the need for transparency in garment and footwear supply chains'.

Cline, E. L. (2012), 'Overdressed: the shockingly high cost of cheap fashion', New York: Portfolio/Penguin Group.

Diabat, A.; Kannan, D.; Mathiyazhagan, K. (2014), 'Analysis of enablers for implementation of sustainable supply chain management'—A textile case. J. Clean. Prod., 83, 391–403. [CrossRef]

Ellen MacArthur Foundation (2017). 'A new textiles economy: redesigning fashion's future', Report https://www.ellenmacarthurfoundation.org/assets/downloads/A-New-Textiles- Economy_Full-Report_Updated_1-12-17.pdf

Euromonitor International (2017). 'Global consumer trends survey'. Available at: https://go.euromonitor.com/white-paper-survey-2017-lifestyles.html

Euromonitor International (2018). 'New consumerism and the search for sustainability'.

Euromonitor International, 2018. Available at: https://blog.euromonitor.com/2018/05/global-apparel-footwear-valued-us-1-7-trillion-2017-millions-of-used-clothing-disposed-every-year.html.

European Commission (2017). "A background analysis on transparency and traceability in the garment value chain', Final Report, September

European Commission (2019). 'Transparency and Sustainability of the EU Risk Assessment in the Food Chain'. Available at: https://ec.europa.eu/food/safety/general_food_law/transparency-and-sustainability-eu-risk-assessment-food-chain_en

European Commission, Regulation (EC) No 1907/2006 of the European Parliament and of the Council (REACH).

European Parliament (2014). 'Workers' conditions in the textile and clothing sector: just an Asian affair? Issues at stake after the Rana Plaza tragedy'. Briefing, August.

European Union (2005). Directive 2005/29/EC of the European Parliament and of the Council of 11 May 2005 concerning unfair business-to-consumer commercial practices in the internal market.

European Union (2011). Textile Regulation (EU) No 1007/2011 on fibre names and related labelling and marking of the fibre composition of textile products.

Fashion United (2015). 'Global fashion industry statistics'. Available at: https://fashionunited.com/global-fashion-industry-statistics (accessed 3 August 2018).

Global Fashion Agenda and Boston Consulting Group (2017). 'Pulse of the fashion industry', Report.

Global Fashion Agenda and Boston Consulting Group (2018). 'Pulse of the Fashion Industry', Report.

GS1, 2012. 'Business process and system requirements for full supply chain traceability'.

GS1 (2012). 'Global Traceability Standard', Issue 1.3.0. Available at: www.gs1.org/docs/gsmp/traceability/Global_Traceability_Standard.pdf.

GS1 (2018). 'Traceability in apparel & general merchandise value proposition'.

Henninger, C. (2015). 'Traceability the new eco-label in the slow-fashion industry? Consumer perceptions and micro-organizations responses', *Sustainability*, 7(5), 6011–6032.

ILO (2018). 'International framework agreements in the food retail, garment and chemicals sectors: Lessons learned from three case studies'. Available at: https://www.ilo.org/sector/Resources/publications/WCMS_631043/lang--en/index.htm

ISO standard on environmental labels and declarations (14021). Available at: https://www.iso.org/standard/66652.html

ITC, Bulletin No 91/2015: Traceability in Food and Agricultural Products. Available at: http://www.intracen.org/Traceability-in-food-and-agri-products/

ITC Trade Map – Market Analysis Tools. Available at: https://marketanalysis.intracen.org/TradeMap.aspx

Kumar, V., Kumar Agrawal, T., Wand, L. & and Yan Chen (2017). 'Contribution of traceability towards attaining sustainability in the textile sector', *Textiles and Clothing Sustainability*, 3(1), 5.

Marconi M., Marilungo E., Papetti P. & Germani M. (2017). 'Traceability as a means to investigate supply chain sustainability: the real case of a leather shoe supply chain', International Journal of Production Research.

Martin, M., (2013). "Creating sustainable apparel value chains: a primer on industry transformation", Impact economy.

McKinsey & Company (2018). 'The state of fashion 2018'. Available at: https://www.mckinsey.com/industries/retail/our-insights/renewed-optimism-for-the-fashion-industry

Nimbalker G., Mawson J., and Cremen C. (2015). 'The truth behind the barcode: Australian fashion report'.

Norton, T., Beier, J., Shields, L., Househam, A., Bombis, E., & Liew, D. (2014). *A Guide to Traceability: A Practical Approach to Advance Sustainability in Global Supply Chains. United Nations Global Compact Office*: New York. Available online at: https://www.unglobalcompact.org/docs/issues_doc/supply_chain/Traceability/Guide_to_Traceability.pdf

OECD, FAO (2016). 'Guidance for responsible agricultural supply chains'.

OECD (2017). 'Due diligence guidance for responsible supply chains in the garment and footwear sector'.
Pal R., Gander J. (2018).'Modelling environmental value: an examination of sustainable business models within the fashion industry' *jJournal of Cleaner Production*, pp. 251-263.
Probst L., Frideres L. & Pedersen B., PwC Luxembourg (2015). 'Traceability across the Value Chain Advanced Tracking Systems Business innovation 1; Case study 40 Business Innovation', Observatory European Commission.
Richero R., Ferrigno S. (2017).'A Background Analysis on Transparency and Traceability in the Garment Value Chain', European Commission, DAI Europe, EPRD
Rose, M. (2014, 30 June). Inspections roil garment industry in Bangladesh. In Taipei Times (p. 9).
Sheng L. (2017). 'Market Size of the Global Textile and Apparel Industry: 2015 to 2020.' FASH455 Global Apparel & Textile Trade and Sourcing (Accessed August 13, 2018). Available at: https://shenglufashion.com/2017/06/06/market-size-of-the-global-textile-and-apparel-industry-2015-to-2020/
Sheng L. (2017), 'WTO Reports World Textile and Apparel Trade in 2016.' FASH455 Global Apparel & Textile Trade and Sourcing (Accessed August 13, 2018) Available at: https://shenglufashion.com/2017/10/12/wto-reports-world-textile-and-apparel-trade-in-2016/
Social Accountability International, SA8000 Standard Avilable at: http://www.sa-intl.org/index.cfm?fuseaction=Page.ViewPage&PageID=1689
Strijbos, B. (2018). 'Global Fashion Industry Statistics - International Apparel'. Fashion United, 15 May. Available at: https://fashionunited.com/global-fashion-industry-statistics (accessed 13 August 2018).
UNECE (2016). 'Traceability for Sustainable Trade: A Framework to design Traceability Systems for Cross Border Trade' (ECE/TRADE/429). Available at: https://www.unece.org/fileadmin/DAM/trade/Publications/ECE_TRADE_429E_TraceabilityForSustainableTrade.pdf.
UNECE (2017). 'Textile4SDG12: Transparency in textile value chains in relation to the environmental, social and human health impacts of parts, components and production processes'.
UN/CEFACT Plenary (2019). Available at: http://www.unece.org/uncefact/25th-plenary.html, April.
WTO (2018). Press Brief: Textiles, Accessed September 19, 2018, retrieved from: https://www.wto.org/english/thewto_e/minist_e/min96_e/textiles.htm.

5 Illegitimate Trade in Fashion and Technologies for Traceability and Supply Chain Protection

by *Iolanda D'Amato*

> *Real happiness is cheap enough,*
> *yet how dearly we pay for its counterfeit.*
> Hosea Ballou

Illegitimate trade and counterfeiting in the fashion industry has increased significantly in recent years, requiring companies to define holistic brand protection strategies and implement new technologies for product authentication and traceability. In order to successfully compete, firms have to distinguish themselves not only on the basis of their product design and marketing activities but they should be able to guarantee a secure, safe and reliable manufacturing and distribution process and to monitor each and every step of their supply chain.

The number of technologies for product authentication, traceability and supply chain protection have been increasing in the last decade and will be even more relevant as we head towards 2030. Technologies such as RFID, NFC and blockchain are transversal to all the activities of the Renewed Fashion Value Chain model. This chapter introduces the risks of illegitimate trade, presents the main pillars of a successful brand protection strategy and classifies the key technologies for product authentication and traceability, discussing the advantages and disadvantages.

5.1 Illegitimate trade and counterfeiting in fashion and luxury

Counterfeiting is defined as 'an unauthorized representation of a registered trademark carried on goods identical or similar to goods for which the trademark is registered, with a view to deceiving the purchaser into believing that he/she is buying the original goods'.[1]

Due to the illegal nature of counterfeiting, it is difficult to provide precise estimates about the losses caused to the economy; quantification becomes available only after seizures at customs. Seizures are not comprehensive of all the circulating counterfeits; in fact, they intercept only around 10% of cross-border illegal trade and do not take into account the number of counterfeit products produced and distributed within a single country.

The OECD estimates that the global trade of counterfeit products is equal to 2.5% of worldwide imports, for a total value of $461 billion, compared with total imports in world trade of $17.9 trillion.[2] Notably, this figure represents an increase of more than 80% over the OECD's findings in 2008.

Fashion and luxury is one of the industries most affected by counterfeiting. This category, including clothing, textiles, footwear, eyewear, handbags and watches, accounts for $98 billion – only within the counterfeiting market. Among fake goods confiscated at customs in the USA, 49.8% are from the fashion industry;[3] in Europe fashion counterfeits equal 58% of the total value of seized fake goods.[4]

According to a recent research paper by the OECD,[5] the four most counterfeited brands globally are Rolex, Nike, Ray-Ban and Louis Vuitton. A similar research by the World Customs Organization (2016) confirms Nike as the primary counterfeited brand in terms of the number of fake units produced.

The counterfeiting phenomenon in the fashion industry is much more complex and interconnected with the legitimate chain than the simple concept of creating a product replica. The LISC model (Figure 10) analyses the interaction between the legitimate and the illegitimate supply chain, that is, the supply chain of counterfeiters. This approach does is not limited to counterfeiting, but instead it includes exhaustively all the phenomena under the umbrella of 'illegitimate trade'.

---

[1] OECD, 2013.
[2] OECD/EUIPO, 2016.
[3] US Customs and Border Protection, 2018.
[4] European Commission, 2017.
[5] OECD, 2018.

Illegitimate trade refers to all activities which touch the illegitimate supply chain for at least one stage of the chain. There are five stages in a typical fashion supply chain: (1) design, (2) production, (3) warehouse, (4) retailer, (5) customer.

Figure 10 LISC model

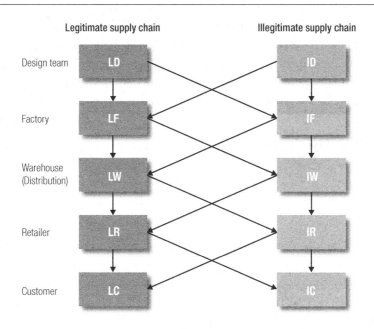

Source: D'Amato and Papadimitriou, 2013.

The model describes seven different phenomena: the product is original and the supply chain legitimate only if the product flows from the design stage to the final customer, without ever touching the illegitimate supply chain (1 – legitimate trade).

The other six possibilities describe six different categories of illegitimate trade. The second category analysed is pure counterfeiting. Pure counterfeiting refers to fakes produced entirely in the illegitimate supply chain, without infiltrating in the legitimate one. This category is not deceptive, as consumers are perfectly aware that goods sold on market stalls are fakes. Then we have 'supply chain infiltrations'. This, the third category of the model, refers to the situation in which a fake product is introduced in the legitimate supply chain and finally sold, as genuine, to a deceived customer.

The scenario of product diversion, the fourth category, occurs when an original product is stolen or diverted – this is the case of parallel or grey markets. The fifth category is represented by factory overruns. In such scenario, legitimate manufacturers agree with the brand owner to produce a predetermined amount of units. However, they decide to produce more than agreed, to sell their surplus stocks to illegitimate players. Category six is retail service copycat: it occurs when the demand for original goods is fulfilled by illegitimate retailers, which copy the format of authentic stores. Finally, shoplifting represents category seven. Shoplifting is simply a theft of authentic products from a legitimate retailer. Once stolen, products are resold via a different channel. An overview of the different categories is provided in Figure 11.

5.2 Countering illegitimate trade and protecting the legitimate supply chain

The complexity of illicit trade in the fashion and luxury industry requires brand owners to be proactive in the fight against counterfeiting. Traditionally, tackling counterfeiting was perceived as an operational activity, involving only the IP and legal department. Instead, nowadays firms have understood the importance of inter-functional cooperation to fight illicit trade. Proactive firms treat anti-counterfeiting as a strategic activity, involving multiple functions at the same time to ensure prevention and repression of counterfeiting. Four activities can contribute in the fight against counterfeiting: 1) marketing and communication, 2) supply chain, 3) legal and IP, 4) innovation and technology.

Marketing and communication activities involve all processes to discourage customers from buying counterfeits and to educate them about the difference between authentic and fake, to increase their awareness of this phenomenon. The final aim of marketing and communication is to decrease the demand for counterfeits.

Concerning supply chain activities, brand owners can leverage on a wide array of tools to reduce the risk of counterfeiting. Supply chain activities involve managing suppliers, outsourcers, distributors and retailers, fostering growth and collaboration.

Figure 11 The LISC model categories

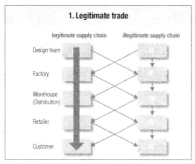
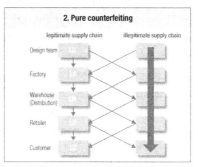
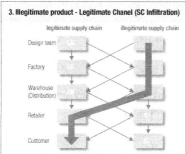

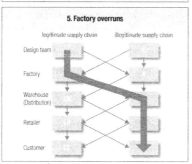

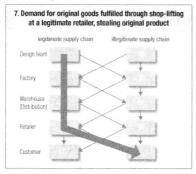

Source: D'Amato and Papadimitriou, 2013.

Starting with the manufacturing process, internalizing or increasing control of this activity would reduce the threat of factory overruns. It may be important to reduce the number of partners, relying on few – but long-term – trusted relationships. Regardless of the type of relationship established, it is fundamental to perform periodic inspections at the supplier's site, and ensure that all scraps and defective products are destroyed. When suppliers need to rely on subcontractors, it is of fundamental importance to limit the number of subcontractors allowed. Indeed, when the layers of partners increase over a certain number, transparency is hindered, and it becomes harder to retain control over the supply chain.

Looking at the downstream supply chain, having in place an exclusive distribution strategy – selling products only through directly operated stores (DOS) – ensures the brand owner can limit problems, such as the emergence of parallel or grey markets. For companies that choose to rely on external distributors, the best practice is to select a few trusted partners, and to periodically verify their operations and to whom they sell. However, retaining control over the last mile of the supply chain is becoming even more complex since the emergence of the online channel.

Legal and IP have a dual role on the prevention side: 1) registering patents and trademarks to protect IP rights, tackling counterfeiting and trademark infringement, and 2) having to work closely with public authorities and governments to detect and block counterfeits and counterfeiters.

Finally, technology and innovation tools are considered increasingly relevant and effective for brand protection strategy and anti-counterfeiting activities. Introducing specific product features, such as authenticity labels, codes and the use of unusual raw materials, increases the complexity of product design and allows tracking and tracing of production and distribution processes. Generally speaking, the more complex these technologies are, the higher the costs for counterfeiters to produce replicas in large amounts.

5.3 Technologies for anti-counterfeiting and brand protection

Ideally, anti-counterfeiting technologies should be simple to apply, difficult to imitate and make the product identifiable. In fact, it is often crucial to evaluate the trade-off between the benefits brought by a greater protection of company products, and the costs of implementing the chosen solutions, of modifying internal and external processes to adopt certain technologies and, more generally, of managing the added complexity stemming from new machinery, processes and controls.

Several solutions are available for authenticating both products and their packaging or labels and for tracking the process and supply chain that they go through; these solutions ensure both the authenticity of the product and the legitimacy of the supply chain – from the production and distribution, down to the sale to consumers.

Most of the available solutions have two common objectives: they enable the company, stakeholders and the authorities to identify counterfeit products and hinder counterfeiters, increasing the necessary investments for them to continue the production and distribution of counterfeit goods.

Available technologies come in a wide range of usability and price, from very affordable and easy-to-deploy solutions, to more powerful mechanisms that may require partial modifications to business processes, depending on the specific requirements of the brand and on the type of products to be protected.

The main technologies can be classified according to the following aspects:

- The role of technology in the company's anti-counterfeiting system
- The visibility of control and anti-counterfeiting elements to end users and to those involved in the authentication process

As far as their role is concerned, technologies can be divided into two main categories: product authentication tools and tools used for product identification and traceability along the supply chain (track and trace). The goal of the former is to identify the product and check its consistency with the accompanying documentation; the latter aims to control the process of a given product to ensure that all the steps followed, from production to distribution, are exactly those planned by the company for that specific good.

Based on the visibility of product authentication technologies, these can be divided into two macro-categories: overt and covert technologies.

Overt technologies are all those technologies that involve the insertion of features or labels on the product, plainly visible to anyone who can directly interact with the product; these are simple to use and are easily understood by people outside of the authorized personnel, allowing even non-experts to distinguish genuine products from fakes, and thus increasing customers' perception of acquiring an authentic product.

Conversely, covert technologies are hidden inside the product or packaging and are invisible. Inserted on products or on the elements to be protected, they require special tools to be read and decrypted by the manufacturing company or the brand owner. In this case, only those who are officially responsible for identifying products and have access to the necessary devices to communicate with the covert technologies inserted on the product can carry out the authenticity verification. Consumers do not have the ability to pinpoint the relevant components inserted inside products, on packaging or on labels, nor to decrypt the data they contain. Various types of anti-counterfeiting technologies and media are commercially available, the most common of which are shown in Table 4.

Table 4 Main technologies for product authentication and track and trace

	Product Authentication	Track and Trace
Covert	• Holograms with hidden codes • Security, latent or smart inks (UV/IR) • Encoded magnetic wires • Micro-elements/Taggants	• RFID (Radio Frequency Identification) • EPC (Electronic Product Code) • NFC (Near-Field Communication) • Blockchain
Overt	• Simple holograms • Colour-shifting inks • Colour-shifting films • Watermarks • Encoded magnetic wires	

Source: Author's own elaboration.

Holograms are three-dimensional images of an object on a photographic plate obtained from the interference of two laser beams, one diffracted by the object and the other reflected by a mirror. The perceived image varies according to the angle at which light hits the hologram; some types of hologram support the insertion of hidden codes that can be revealed using dedicated readers.

Inks enable users to view some features and information printed on the packaging or directly on the products. Again, there are various types of inks: the simplest, which are visible to the naked eye, change colour or become fluorescent depending on the angle at which the packaging is viewed. Usually, consumers will notice this colour effect by changing the viewing angle of the object.

Other types of inks, such as 'latent' or 'intelligent' ones, are not visible to the naked eye but require triggers to activate them, such as temperature, UV light, infrared light, or specific detectors such as polarized screens.

Watermarks are still one of the most popular security features today, and are easily verified and used in banknotes, cheque books and documents. It is a paper-making process that enables a desired shape to be seen on the paper when viewed against the light.

Encoded magnetic wires are polyester strips on which magnetic metal oxides are deposited, generating dipoles with a defined magnetic orientation. Letters or numbers are inserted on micro-engraved wires using de-metallization, screen printing or laser techniques, while plastic micro-particles that are reactive to UV light are glued onto wires with encoded micro-engraved elements.

Encoded magnetic wires can be inserted directly into the fabric during manufacturing and are normally placed in specific locations to make sure they are present in each item produced. Multi-coloured fibres, visible to the naked eye (overt) or revealed by UV light (covert), can be incorporated into paper or plastic. Fibres can also be encrypted (forensic).

Micro-elements are micro- or nano-particles inserted into the raw material (plastic, glass or liquids) or applied to the surface of various materials. Their detection, which requires the use of specialized devices, guarantees the authenticity of the material. These devices can determine the spatial position of individual particles, giving each object a unique identity.

While overt and covert technologies focus on product authentication, track and trace technologies do not limit their scope to product authentication but are able to 'authenticate' the end-to-end process – the product's supply chain.

This is why they are considered the real technological breakthrough to tackle counterfeiting. These technologies combine a centralized database with a hardware device attached to each product, and allow them to be tracked throughout the supply chain. In this way, companies can tell with almost absolute certainty the provenance of each good. Examples of those technologies are RFID (radio frequency identification), EPC (electronic product code), NFC (near-field communication) tags and blockchain.

RFID systems are technologies that use electromagnetic communication to exchange data between a terminal (the RFID reader) and an object (the RFID tag) with the aim of identifying the product and verifying the process it has undergone.

Compared to barcodes, RFID tags allow for more information to be stored, can be read at a greater distance, and additional information can be added later on, at any point during the product or label life cycle. For this reason, RFID technology, initially used in production, warehousing and logistics processes, has also proved particularly useful as an authentication tool in the scope of anti-counterfeiting and a method of interacting with final customers. EPCs replace EAN codes in a digital world.

Although the technology still has a number of limitations related to the cost and complexity of implementation as well as privacy issues for final customers, it seems that in recent years, adoption has increased in several sectors, especially driven by the greater omnichannel experience that the use of RFID could bring.

The versatility of the technology represents both one of the main limitations and strengths of this technology. Its implementation into end-to-end supply chain processes allows for a number of benefits in terms of process speed and reliability, error reduction and greater integration throughout the supply chain. It also makes it possible to guarantee the legitimacy of products and the processes, and to manage after-sales activities and warranties. However, a project that touches on so many aspects and involves so many company departments is challenging; it shakes up the company, its organization and its way of working. To be carried out, it needs to be part of the company's strategic plan, which is very rarely the case.

Conversely, when RFID Technology is used only in certain departments, on certain specific processes or product lines without actually reaching a 'critical mass' (either in terms of quantity of tagged products or in terms of degree of process coverage), it carries the risk of making things more complicated because of the resulting poor integration with existing systems, processes and organization. On the contrary, the major advantages of the technology are linked to its transversality and to the synergies deriving from extensive adoption.

Although the various technologies have been listed in an alternative way in order to highlight their peculiar aspects and main differences, a complete anti-counterfeiting solution requires the simultaneous use of more than one tool on a given product in order to satisfy different authentication and confidentiality needs.

In particular, the simultaneous use of overt and covert technologies of varying complexity allows not only to give a series of information to consumers – creating at the same time loyalty towards the product and allowing them to distinguish genuine products thanks to overt technologies – but also to make potential controls by authorized personnel possible, perhaps providing for a different level of escalation.

Finally, blockchain represents the most 'trendy' of the track and trace technologies, although its application can offer so much more than this. Blockchain is a type of distributed ledger, which is an expanding, chronologically ordered list of cryptographically signed, irrevocable transactional records shared by all participants in a network. Each record contains a time stamp and reference links to the previous transactions. With this information, anyone with access rights can trace a transactional event at any point in its history, belonging to any participant. Blockchain and other distributed-ledger technologies provide trust algorithmically in untrusted environments, eliminating the need for a trusted central authority.

Among its benefits, the technology can support companies in creating transparent and immutable supply chain traceability systems, controlling distribution partners and monitoring the grey market, improving customer loyalty, increasing customer lifetime value and establishing a direct connection with clients independently of the sales channel. The immutability of the database can ensure in almost 100% of the cases the provenance of goods. In addition, this technology creates additional benefits for sustainable firms which want to open up their supply chain, sharing full transparency with their customers about the raw materials utilized and working conditions for their employees, and it is considered as one of the most promising technologies to prevent fraud and counterfeiting.

Box 12 presents an example of blockchain implementation.

Box 12 Martine Jarlgaard and blockchain implementation

Martine Jarlgaard London (MJL) was founded in 2013 by Danish born, London-based designer MJ, who had previously worked for brands such as Vivienne Westwood, All Saints and Diesel. MJL is a UK-based fashion tech-lab working on the intersection between sustainability, technology, fashion, science and art.

From 2013 to 2016, the company manufactured and distributed high-end fashion clothes experimenting with concepts around sustainability. To ensure product longevity and quality, the MJL pieces were made from premium sustainable, European materials, mainly from Italy and France, where Martine Jarlgaard collaborated directly with the best quality mills. Early MJL pieces were distributed through specialized e-commerce platforms.

From its launch, MJL has distinguished itself on two pillars: attention to sustainability and use of new technologies. The company was one of the first to introduce blockchain technology, AR and VR.

MJL does not present collections in the traditional way; the firm relies on technology to create futuristic projects in order to push the way we think about the future of fashion and to interact more closely with customers while fostering 'brand storytelling'. With this purpose in mind, MJL presented the world's first mixed-reality fashion show in September 2016, at London Fashion Week: leveraging AR.

During this experience visitors experienced the MJL collection which was made from waste materials, certified sustainable and organic materials. The MJL pieces were shown through 3D holograms, encouraging visitors to engage through exploration and curiosity as a contrast to the more passive experience of the conventional catwalk show.

In 2017, MJL implemented blockchain in its supply chain. The aim of the blockchain application was to engage consumers, and to empower(ing) them to make well-informed purchasing decisions, by having access to transparency and information about product and manufacturing process. This was the first ever Blockchain-powered supply chain transparency fashion pilot.

When applied to the supply chain of physical products, blockchain allows validation of each step of the production process, from sourcing of raw materials to delivery to the final point of sale, ensuring maximum transparency for customers.

More specifically, the product is given a digital history through a NFC tag. This is the product's 'digital twin', which allows the firm and customers to track, trace and verify its origin. The smart label assigns a unique ID to each garment, which contains specific data (mapping, content and timestamps) that have been recorded in real-time for every step of the production process. At the moment of purchase, consumers can scan the NFC tag through their smartphone, to gain access to the product's supply chain journey.

The first product utilising blockchain technology was the MJL Alpaca Mirror Jumper. When scanning the tag, consumers are shown a brief introduction of the product, along with the date of production and the batch ID. This provides access to two sections: 'Info' and 'Journey'. The different suppliers involved in the production process (from raw materials to the end product) are presented and described; as well as the materials used, and product claims. In the 'Journey' section, the different stages of the supply chain have been illustrated. In the case of the MJL Alpaca Mirror Jumper, the supplier information of the raw materials which consist of white alpaca fibre and a black alpaca fibre and the raw material transactions were logged on Blockchain in real-time on 12 April. Following this stage the asset (the alpaca fleece) was then transferred to the second member of the supply chain. Once the raw materials have been spun into the alpaca yarn, this was then transferred to the last actor of the production process on 28 April. Finally the MJL Alpaca Mirror Jumper was completed on 2 May and then transferred to Martine Jarlgaard London.

Today MJL does not focus on traditional fashion business models such as manufacturing and selling fashion items. Instead MJL is challenging the fashion industry and continues to work with innovation, sustainability and technology through visionary, avant-garde projects.

In addition to working in the field of 'Future of Fashion' Martine Jarlgaard created and launched MEET YOURSELF in 2017. MEET YOURSELF is a Mixed Reality art installation and experience where you get to MEET YOURSELF. The concept evolves around self-perception, human psychology, mental health, consumption and our future with technology, alternative realities and avatars. The experience of MEET YOURSELF involves being 3D scanned, and through the Microsoft HoloLens or Magic Leap headset getting to stand face to face with your lifesize, 3D, holographic avatar of yourself. MEET YOURSELF was launched with the support of Unity Technologies and shown at Louisiana Museum of Modern Art in 2018. MEET YOURSELF is a way to challenge your "self-perception" and to create a real out of body experience, giving you the opportunity to see ourselves as others do.

In the current fashion landscape of overflowing landfills and too many garments being treated as disposable, MEET YOURSELF has the ambition of creating an impactful experience, which challenges the way in which we consume as well as questioning the idea of value as we know it in order to help us dematerialise consumption which represents one of the greatest challenges surrounding UN Global Goals SDG12.

Sources: Bunnis, 2016; Martine Jarlgaard London (2018).

References

Arthur, R. (2017). 'From farm to finished garment: blockchain is aiding this fashion collection with transparency'. *Forbes*. Available at: https://www.forbes.com/sites/rachelarthur/2017/05/10/garment-blockchain-fashion-transparency/#5e3bc18a74f3 (accessed 17 July 2018).

Berman, B. (2008). 'Strategies to detect and reduce counterfeiting activity'. *Business Horizons*, 51(3), 191–199.

Bunnis, M. (2016). 'Interview with Martine Jarlgaard – Fashion Feature'.

1883magazine.com. Available at: http://www.1883magazine.com/features/features/martine-jarlgaard (accessed 17 July 2018).

Chen, L., Yue, T. & Zhao, X. (2018). '8 ways brands can fight counterfeits in China'. *Harvard Business Review*. Available at: https://hbr.org/2018/05/8-ways-brands-can-fight-counterfeits-in-china (accessed 17 July 2018).

D'Amato, I. (2016). *La filiera del vero. Contraffazione e autenticità dei prodotti Made in Italy* (1st ed.). Milan, Egea.

D'Amato, I. & Papadimitriou, T. (2013). 'Legitimate vs illegitimate: The luxury supply chain and its doppelganger'. *International Journal of Retail & Distribution Management*, 41(11/12), 986–1007.

Li, L. (2013). 'Technology designed to combat fakes in the global supply chain'. *Business Horizons*, 56(2), 167–177.

Martine Jarlgaard London (2018). 'About Us'. Available at: http://martinejarlgaard.com/About (accessed 17 July 2018).

OECD/EUIPO (2018). *Trade in Counterfeit and Pirated Goods: Mapping the Economic Impact*. Paris, OECD Publishing.

Wilcox, A.E. & Boys, K.A. (2014). 'Reduce product counterfeiting: An integrated approach'. *Business Horizons*, 57(2), 279–288.

6 Managing Circularity in Fashion

by *Francesca Romana Rinaldi and Elisabetta Amadei*

> *Nothing is created, nothing is destroyed,*
> *everything is transformed.*
> Antoine-Laurent de Lavoisier

The system which currently dominates industrial production is defined as 'cradle to grave', a process which follows a linear and one-way business model: resources are extracted, processed into a product, sold and finally eliminated, buried in a kind of 'grave', usually an incinerator. The cradle-to-cradle approach aims at creating a 'closed circle' which, instead of ending with disposal, considers the waste product as a nourishing factor to be reincorporated in a 'continuous closed cycle' without any energy or physical materials being wasted. In general, the principle suggests that any decision may not be the correct one if we only consider one part of the product's life cycle: in order to be truly environmentally friendly we must begin with an analysis that determines the environmental impact of every stage, from production, to usage, recycling and disposal. The circular approach is transversal to all the activities of the Renewed Fashion Value Chain model. In this chapter the findings of the most up-to-date reports on circular textiles and clothing will be presented, underlining the opportunities and challenges of circularity in fashion.

6.1 The need for circularity

6.1.1 *Definition of circularity*

An economic system can be defined as 'circular' when products and services are traded in a closed loop, creating a virtuous circle capable of prospering and regenerating. The Ellen MacArthur Foundation provides one of the most credited definitions of circular economy:

> Looking beyond the current take-make-waste extractive industrial model, a circular economy aims to redefine growth, focusing on positive society-wide benefits. It entails gradually decoupling economic activity from the consumption of finite resources and designing waste out of the system. [...] The circular model builds economic, natural, and social capital.[1]

Our industrial economy is based on a linear model of resource consumption: companies collect and extract raw materials in order to manufacture and sell products that the consumers will dispose of once they are no longer able to satisfy their needs. This model leads to extensive quantities of waste, vast damages to ecosystems and higher exposure to risks (mainly related to resource prices and supply disruptions) for companies. All these negative effects are emphasized by predicted world demographic trends. A report from the McKinsey Global Institute estimates that by 2030, there will be 3 billion more middle-class consumers in the global economy.[2]

One of the first-born manifestos calling for a radical change in the industry is *Cradle-to-Cradle: Remaking the Way We Make Things* by William McDonough and Michael Braungart. This 2002 book calls for a disruptive change in the economy: a switch from a linear cradle-to-grave approach to a circular cradle-to-cradle[3] one. In a cradle-to-cradle economy, products are conceived from the very outset with a smart design, keeping in mind that along the way they will need to be recycled, as either 'biological' or 'technical' nutrients (see Figure 12).

The key to a sustainable future does not lie exclusively in simply holding the products for longer; waste needs to become nutrients and raw materials for further manufacturing. Obsolescence is no longer a problem in one

---

[1] https://www.ellenmacarthurfoundation.org/circular-economy/concept.
[2] McKinsey Global Institute, 2011.
[3] The certification program is based on the Cradle to Cradle Design™ framework and methodology, which has been developed and implemented by MBDC over the past two decades. MBDC created the Cradle to Cradle Certified™ Products Program to recognize achievement in applying Cradle to Cradle Design principles. Cradle to Cradle Certified™ is a registered trademark of the Cradle to Cradle Products Innovation Institute, which administers the certification program as an independent, third-party standard.

respect: companies need to develop new policies to recycle old products, using innovation as their main tool.

Figure 12 Technical and biological cycle in the Cradle to Cradle Design™ Framework

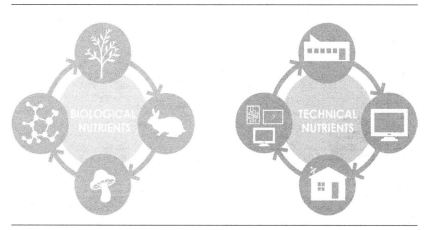

Source: Cradle to Cradle.

6.1.2 *The need for circularity in fashion*

As highlighted in the report 'A New Textiles Economy', between 2000 and 2015 the production of clothes has doubled, given the growth of the population, the per capita expenditure and the affirmation of the fast fashion phenomenon that offers numerous collections per year at a reduced price.

Figure 13 illustrates the alarming increase in the sale of clothing and the simultaneous decrease in the use of the garments.

The current system operates in a linear manner, that is, a large amount of non-renewable resources is used for the production of clothing that will be used for a short period of time and then it will be thrown away, sent to landfill or burned. It is estimated that over $500 billion of value is lost due to underuse and lack of garment recycling. The take-make-dispose model has innumerable negative impacts, both social and environmental: the main ones being gas and CO_2 emissions, the use of substances that

Figure 13 Growth of clothing sales and decline in clothing utilization since

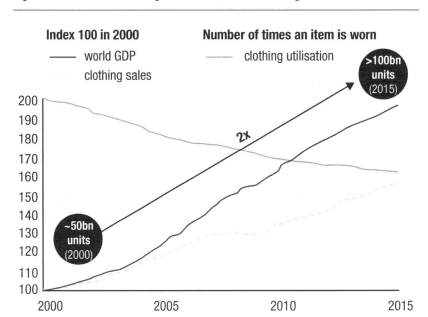

Source: Ellen MacArthur Foundation, 2017, "A New Textile Economy", https://www.ellenmacarthurfoundation.org

are harmful to the health of workers, consumers and the environment and ocean pollution.[4]

Hence the need for a 'New Textiles Economy' based on the principles of the circular economy, an economy in which garments, fabrics and fibres maintain their value during the entire use and can be reintroduced into the supply chain after their employment, never becoming waste. This economy, which is already being primarily supported by institutions (see Box 13), makes it possible to achieve better economic, social and environmental results.

[4] Ellen MacArthur Foundation, 2017.

> **Box 13** The UN and European Commission support of circular economy
>
> The SDGs (see chapter 2, paragraph 2.3),[5] as a substantial part of the 2030 Agenda, are a group of 17 global goals defined by the United Nations General Assembly in 2015, setting objectives to be reached by 2030. Each SDG is broad based and interdependent; each has a list of targets that are measured with indicators. Through the SDG tracker, a free, open access website publication,[6] it is possible to track progress towards all the different SDGs. The circular economy holds particular promise for achieving multiple SDGs, especially SDG 6 on water, 7 on energy, 12 on sustainable consumption and production, 13 on climate change, 14 on oceans and 15 on life on land.
>
> In 2015, the European Commission adopted an action plan to help accelerate Europe's transition towards a circular economy, boost global competitiveness, promote sustainable economic growth and generate new jobs.[7] The action plan sets out 54 measures to 'close the loop' of product life cycles: from production and consumption to waste management and the market for secondary raw materials. All the measures under the action plan have now been completed or are being implemented, as stated by the Report from the Commission to the European Parliament drawn up in Brussels in March 2019. The EU monitoring Framework for the Circular Economy shows that the transition has helped put the EU back on a path of job creation while opening up new business opportunities, giving rise to new business models and the development of new markets.[8]

6.1.3 *The benefits of circular fashion*

Figure 14 illustrates the environmental impact of a traditional garment or accessory for each stage of the product life cycle and its indirect impact on working conditions safety.

Circular fashion should generate several benefits for businesses, environment, citizens and society, for many reasons. According to Euromonitor International (2016), thanks to circular economy, a company can manage to:

1. reduce supply risks, given the resource scarcity;
2. increase the sustainability quotient;
3. meet the needs given by the regulation;

---

[5] https://www.un.org/sustainabledevelopment/sustainable-development-goals/.
[6] https://sdg-tracker.org/.
[7] https://ec.europa.eu/commission/priorities/jobs-growth-and-investment/towards-circular-economy_en.
[8] European Commission, 2019.

Figure 14 The impact of a fashion item on environment and the working conditions safety

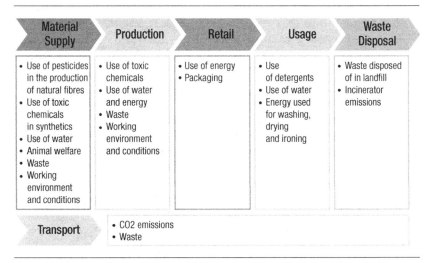

Source: Adapted from Draper, Murray and Weissbrod, 2007, and Rinaldi and Testa, 2014

4. achieve cost savings, thanks to the reduction of raw material costs;
5. increase the innovation quotient, also as a strategy to differentiation for shareholders and consumers;
6. meet the consumer demand, given the increase in the environmental awareness.

In order to achieve those benefits, it is crucial to innovate the business model in every activity of the Renewed Fashion Value Chain, starting from the design phase (see Box 14).

Box 14 The principles of eco-design for circularity

Following an interview with Silvia Giovanardi, eco-efficient fashion designer, founder of Silvia Giovanardi and co-founder of WRÅD, the main principles of eco-design for circularity in fashion are:

- Engagement of 'win-win' situations between companies (i.e. I take your waste for free to use it as a raw material for my production, and you don't have to pay for its disposal);

- Transformation of industrial waste into new value (i.e. in nature the concept of waste does not exist);
- Reduction of the usage of precious resources (e.g. water) and of the toxic chemicals (dangerous for producers as well as wearers);
- Awareness of every consequence of each step;
- Wise production in terms of quantities (i.e. the obligation to over-produce is harmful and alienates the passion to create) to avoid wasting resources;
- Never-ending research, even when we think we have found the best way to apply circular economy and its principles;
- Long-term vision of the potential reuse of the material we are saving from a dead end (i.e. not only in its second life, but eventually in infinite lives).

The main challenges to apply these principles of eco-design for circularity in fashion lie in the capability to keep in our minds all the main principles of circularity at the same time, because the choice to apply just one of them, in a partly compromised chain, could be a waste of effort, energy and time, and it could destroy our WHY.[9]

6.2 Circular fashion: main principles and models

According to the Ellen MacArthur Foundation, every second, the equivalent of one rubbish truck of textiles is burned or added to landfill. The textile industry has also been identified as a major contributor to oceans' pollution: washing clothes releases half a million tonnes of plastic microfibres into the ocean every year (the equivalent of roughly 50 billion plastic bottles). It is clear that today's linear system uses large amounts of resources while having a strong negative impact on the environment. A circular approach is the answer to preserve the natural capital and ensure sustainable development.

In recent years, brands and retail companies in the fashion industry have started to rethink their business and redesign their strategies, procedures and supply chains. In doing so, they have shaped their business models following those that characterized circular economy, in accordance with three principles:[10]

---

[9] Some suggested reading to further explore the concept of eco-design for circularity include: Minney, 2011; Korn, 2012; Klanten and Bohle, 2012.
[10] Ellen MacArthur Foundation – https://www.ellenmacarthurfoundation.org/.

1. Preserve and enhance natural capital by controlling finite stocks and balancing renewable resource flows: regenerate, virtualize, exchange;
2. Optimize resource yields by circulating products, components and materials in use at the highest utility at all times in both technical and biological cycles: regenerate, share, optimize, loop;
3. Foster system effectiveness by revealing and designing out negative externalities throught all the actions mentioned in the first two principles.

The circular economy system 'butterfly' diagram (see Figure 15), designed by the Ellen MacArthur Foundation in partnership with consultants from McKinsey, shows two types of materials flow: 'biological nutrients', that are designed to re-enter the biosphere while building natural capital, and 'technical nutrients' which are designed to circulate in closed loops and never re-enter the biosphere.

Figure 15 Circular economy system 'butterfly' diagram

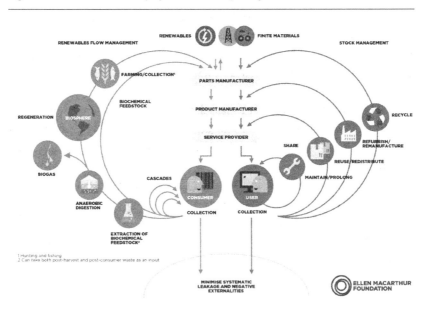

Source: Ellen MacArthur Foundation, 2019, *Circular Economy Systems Diagram*, https://www.ellenmacarthurfoundation.org. Drawing based on Braungart & McDonough, Cradle to Cradle (C2C).

Consumption happens only in biological cycles, where food and biologically based materials are designed to feed back into the system through processes like composting and anaerobic digestion. These cycles regenerate living systems, such as soil, which provide renewable resources for the economy.[11]

Technical cycles recover and restore products, components and materials through different strategies as reported in the Figure 15. First of all, technical nutrients (materials, manufactured products etc.) can be kept in closed loops through 'maintenance'. It is also possible to 'reuse' a product or simply 'redistribute' it through second-hand shops, online and offline. Meanwhile, when some faulty product components need to be replaced, and the product is brought back to a performance state close to the initial one, this is termed 'refurbish or remanufacture'. The final option is 'recycling', but since smaller inner loops retain the highest value, all the previously explained options are preferable to the latter.

Some companies already rely on and apply the 'Butterfly' diagram principles, with a focus on the following activities:

- 'Recycle': recycling and upcycling best practices such as those of Patagonia (Box 15), 'Orange Fiber' (Box 16), WRÅD (Box 17), Progetto Quid (Box 18), MUD Jeans and Eileen Fisher;
- 'Refurbish/remanufacture': product life extension though maintenance and remanufacturing, such as in the case of Patagonia and MUD Jeans;
- 'Reuse/redistribute/maintain/prolong': some of the best practices for what concerns collaborative consumption platforms are Rent the Runway, Vestiaire Collective, Patagonia and MUD Jeans.

The first two activities 'recycle' and 'refurbish/remanufacture' will be analysed below, whereas the other activities will be considered in further detail in Chapter 7, which is fully dedicated to so-called collaborative consumption.

---

[11] Ellen MacArthur Foundation: https://www.ellenmacarthurfoundation.org.

Box 15 Patagonia 360° circularity approach

Patagonia's circularity approach begins with the use of recycled fibers.
"We began making recycled polyester from plastic soda bottles in 1993–the first outdoor clothing manufacturer to transform trash into fleece. It was a positive step toward a more sustainable system–one that uses fewer resources, discards less and better protects people's health.
Today, we recycle used soda bottles, unusable manufacturing waste and worn-out garments (including our own) into polyester fibers to produce clothing. And we offer recycled polyester in a lot more garments, including Capilene® baselayers, shell jackets, board shorts and fleece.
Using recycled polyester lessens our dependence on petroleum as a source of raw materials. It curbs discards, thereby prolonging landfill life and reducing toxic emissions from incinerators. It helps to promote new recycling streams for polyester clothing that is no longer wearable. And it causes less air, water and soil contamination compared to using nonrecycled polyester."[12]
The company's circularity approach is also implemented in the company's commitment to Product life extension through the Worn Wear program, more specifically through Repair & Care Guides and the Reuse & Recycle activities.

Worn Wear
"One of the most responsible things we can do as a company is to make high-quality stuff that lasts for years and can be repaired, so you don't have to buy more of it. The Worn Wear program celebrates the stories we wear, keeps your gear in action longer and provides an easy way to recycle Patagonia garments when they're beyond repair."[13]

Repair & Care Guides
"As individual consumers, the single best thing we can do for the planet is to keep our stuff in use longer."[14]

Reuse & Recycle
"Using Patagonia's $20 Million & Change investment fund, we're supporting new economies that revolve around extending the life of stuff we already own. For example, our partners at Yerdle make it easy to give away things you don't need, and get something useful in return.
And we sell used Patagonia clothing at our Portland retail store through an innovative trade-in program. But nothing lasts forever, so we continue to offer easy ways to recycle Patagonia products—100% of what we make—when they finally reach the end of their useful lives and can no longer be repaired."[15]

---

[12] https://www.patagonia.com.au/pages/recycled-polyester
[13] https://www.patagonia.com.au/pages/worn-wear
[14] https://www.patagonia.com/worn-wear-repairs
[15] https://eu.patagonia.com/it/en/reuse-recycle.html

6.2.1 *Recycling, upcycling and downcycling*[16]

Recycling and upcycling have become buzzwords: a simple definition is needed in order to understand better how to term the different circular activities in a fashion company. Recycling and upcycling are related to the concept of eco-effectiveness, which proposes the 'transformation of products and their associated material flows such that they form a supportive relationship with ecological systems and future economic growth.

The goal is not to minimize the cradle-to-grave flow of materials, but to generate cyclical, cradle-to-cradle "metabolisms" that enable materials to maintain their status as resources and accumulate intelligence over time, i.e. upcycling'.[17] Downcycling is related to a linear system, where 'eco-efficient techniques seek to minimize the volume, velocity, and toxicity of the material flow system, but are incapable of altering its linear progression. Some materials are recycled, but often as an end-of-pipe solution, since these materials are not designed to be recycled. Instead of true recycling, this process is actually downcycling, a downgrade in material quality, which limits usability and maintains the linear, cradle-to-grave dynamic of the material flow system'.[18]

Summing-up:

- *Recycling* – the recycling process is a continuum of varying degrees of down- and upcycling. The general requirement is that 'the collected material should be able to be separated into its component materials using a proven, financially viable process. It should not remain as an inseparable mixture of different materials.
- *Upcycling* – a recycling process that increases the quality and economic value of a material or product.
- *Downcycling* – a recycling process that reduces the quality and economic value of a material or product.

---

[16] https://www.ellenmacarthurfoundation.org/assets/downloads/insight/Circularity Indicators_Methodology_May2015.pdf
[17] Ellen MacArthur Foundation, 2012 - https://www.ellenmacarthurfoundation.org/news/efficiency-vs-effectiveness
[18] Ellen MacArthur Foundation, 2012 - https://www.ellenmacarthurfoundation.org/news/efficiency-vs-effectiveness

Box 16 Interview with Enrica Arena, co-founder Orange Fiber

How and when Orange Fiber was born?
Our adventure started at the end of 2011 in Milan, when we were finishing our studies and sharing a flat. Adriana Santanocito was studying fashion design and she was focusing on innovative and sustainable products while I wanted to get a job in line with my idea of sustainable development and social entrepreneurship. We had different backgrounds, but we shared the dream of changing the world starting from our country – Italy – and region – Sicily – using our skills and passion. Adriana, with her background in design, while writing her thesis, asked the crazy question: what if we could turn citrus juice into an innovative fabric, contributing to the solution of two problems – the environmental and economic impact of citrus juice leftover disposal and the need for sustainable materials in the fashion industry – at one time? Just in Italy, 700,000 tons of citrus byproducts have to be disposed each year. She started testing her hypothesis in the lab with Politecnico di Milano's material chemistry department, and found that it was feasible, so she decided to file for patent and to apply to a startup competition to see how the market would respond to her idea. At that point, she brought me on board, and together we started working to find resources to develop the concept.

What have been the most important developments and turning points that allowed your project to grow and prosper?
Following a collaboration with Politecnico di Milano, an innovative process has been developed that allows more than 700,000 tonnes of byproduct that the citrus processing industry produces every year in Italy (and that would otherwise have to be disposed of with costs for the processing industry and the environment) to be turned into a high-quality fabric that can respond to the need for sustainability and innovation of fashion brands. The innovative process was patented in Italy in 2013 and extended to international PCT the following year. The first prototypes of fabric from citrus juice byproduct were presented in 2014 at the Expo Gate of Milan on the occasion of Vogue Fashion's Night Out. The trademark was registered, and the textile market tested by identifying important strategic partners in the supply chain developing today in Italy and abroad. The first pilot plant for the extraction of pulp from citrus was opened in December 2015 in Sicily. The very first fashion collection made with the exclusive 'Orange Fiber' fabric was launched on the occasion of Earth Day, 22 April 2017, by Salvatore Ferragamo – one of Italy's top fashion brands and a world leader in the luxury industry – in a collaboration that represents the shared ethical values underlying the project, shaping the fabric and showcasing its potential for elegant and sustainable applications. In 2019, H&M included Orange Fiber in the Conscious Exclusive 2019, the premium H&M collection made only with recycled and sustainable materials. In line with its commitment to a greener fashion industry and always attentive to industry innovations, the Swedish brand has chosen Orange Fiber to create a sophisticated boho-style top, a tribute

to the beauty of Nature. Innovation and design come together in this collection that follows the growth path of our company, begun with the victory of the Global Change Award of the H&M Foundation in 2015, and marks a new goal for us and for the future of fashion.

How expensive is it to apply the principles of circularity to a business model?
It really depends on which level of innovation is required by the implementation of the sustainability within the business model. Sustainable innovation is a cost – the industrial process is expensive, as well as the machinery and the R&D – but it is also a very big opportunity, the opportunity to make better the way we all design, produce and consume.

What are the funding opportunities for circular start-ups?
Fundraising for startups and SMEs that operate in the field of sustainability and circularity is harder than for digital companies. Circularity takes time and, actually, there is not a standard frame to which to refer, for this reason the investments (public and private) in this sector are meagre. Recently, things have been changing and more and more there are impact investors that are showing up on the market. This new movement of impact investors is changing the rules, redesigning new opportunities for circular start-ups.

What is your experience with crowdfunding?
Our first experience with crowdfunding dates back to 2014, when we launched a crowdfunding campaign through the TIM Working Capital platform to raise funds to move forward in the R&D process on the vitamin enrichment of our fabrics through nanotechnology. It was a totally new platform; no community was there, and the goal has not been reached. In April 2019 we launched an equity crowdfunding campaign on CrowdFundMe, the first Italian crowdfunding platform listed on the stock exchange with a very large community of professional investors – more than 10,000 followers. This campaign opens up the door of our company to new members, offering the opportunity to small and professional investors to invest in innovation and sustainability, the two crucial sectors for the economy of the future and the two pillars of our company.

What are your future goals? Is the production model that you designed replicable/expandable?
Recently we launched an equity crowdfunding campaign to raise funds to buy machinery to increase our production capacity and meet the demand of fashion brands. At the same time, we are working hard to move forward in the R&D process to a point where we can scale up the technology and restart the production, with a long-term goal to optimize the costs of production. This is crucial to develop new potential collaborations with fashion brands sharing our values and eventually replicate the technology in Italy and abroad, as we extended our

IP in the USA, and it is pending in EU, India, Brazil and Mexico. Expanding our production outside Europe will allow us to increase our impact and minimize our logistics, keeping in mind our sustainability goal. For the future we hope to establish ourselves as the first Italian mover in the segment of sustainable fabrics through 'green' production of cellulosic fabrics from renewable sources and to create a highly recognizable textile brand for its commitment toward environmental protection and transparency.

6.2.2 Product life extension

Every time that we throw away a product, we are losing all the energy and resources that went into its production. Extending the life of products and their components through maintenance and remanufacturing is both highly resource and energy efficient.[19] To facilitate product life extension, rapid replacement cycles need to be avoided and products need to be developed to endure. Remanufacturing a product could mean rebuilding, repairing or restoring it in order to meet or exceed the original equipment manufacturer's (OEM) performance specifications. Maintenance, on the other hand, is a critical activity carried out in the use phase of the product life cycle in order to prolong it and keep the condition and performance of the product intact for as long as possible.

Box 17 Interview with Matteo Ward, co-founder and CEO of WRÅD

How was the idea of WRÅD born and how did it evolve?
WRÅD was born as a purpose-led movement in 2015 with a focused mission: inspiring the market to manifest intangible social and environmental values through tangible in order to catalyse change. The idea of the brand name WRÅD came from an early observation of the status quo in the sustainable fashion segment back in 2014, which was still very raw but lacked some radically innovative excitement around it. WRÅD is thus the synthesis of the words 'RAW' and 'RAD' but also our call to action – because it is only by sparking a short-circuit between the raw, natural world and radical innovation that we can create magic and catalyse real disruptive change.

WRÅD was co-founded by me, Victor Santiago and Silvia Giovanardi. The three of us all have experience and awareness about the true impact of clothing after work-

---

[19] https://circulareconomy.europa.eu/platform/en/good-practices/product-life-extension-through-remanufacturing-europe.

ing in the industry with some big corporations in the retail and luxury segments. In a nutshell, we couldn't really cope any longer with the fact that we were unwillingly contributing to making the fashion industry one of the most polluting worldwide. Upon gradual discovery of the real impact of clothing manufacturing, we grew increasingly frustrated with our corporate roles and were shocked by the fact that nobody, not even within the industry, really knew anything about it. There was – and still is – a huge information asymmetry in regard to the true cost of fashion: a fact that became our first real motivation to quit our corporate jobs and dedicate ourselves to finding ways to generate awareness, because people care when they know and have the power to revolutionze things when they are empowered to do so with knowledge. So, our first entrepreneurial project initially aimed at building the WRÅD purpose and identity by focusing on communication on social media to inspire a new order of social and environmental activistim in Europe. After creating the WRÅD community, at the beginning of 2016 we started developing a uniquely sustainable, circular and smarter mineral-dyeing technique with Italian partners Alisea Recycled and Reused Objects Design (www.alisea.it) and ItalDenim (http://www.italdenim.com). This process, inspired by an ancient Roman dyeing technique, is today patented by Alisea and known as g_pwdr technology.

The final step for us was finding the tangible products through which people, our community, could at this point manifest their 'WRÅD' identity, their desire to become part of the solution and act responsibly for our planet and people. So, we started designing products with purpose, one of which – GRAPHI-TEE™ Endorsed by Perpetua – was recognized, for its sustainable and innovative DNA, as Best of the Best Design Product of the Year at the RedDot Design Award 2017.

What is the final scope, and which are the principles that inspire you and your team in your everyday actions and communication strategies?
WRÅD today is a focus design company dedicated to designing services to catalyse positive change through its own R&D programme for sustainable innovation, its sustainable consultancy and communications branch, an educational programme and its own fashion design brand. WRÅD's diversified activities, motivated by a unifying purpose, are based on three fundamental pillars: educate, innovate, liberate through design.

How does the innovative g_pwdr technology work? What are the environmental benefits?
g_pwdr technology is based on the upcycling of graphite powder, a waste product generated by the manufacture of graphite electrodes. The powder we repurpose is made into liquid form in a water-based solution and then, through an innovative process, it is used it to dye fabrics. g_pwdr technology allows us to give extra value to the products because of the particular service it offers for: 1) The environ-

ment: graphite powder, if not repurposed, is thrown in landfill, making soil sterile, something we can avoid (through the endorsed by Perpetua programme to date, 17 tonnes of graphite powder has been recovered). Moreover, because of the specific properties of graphite, the-use water footprint of the dyeing stage is reduced by 90%; 2) Individual health: Graphite is non-toxic, so our skin is not exposed to toxic chemicals (the UN estimates that 8% of all skin diseases are caused by toxic fabrics); and 3) Society: The process is inspired by an ancient miners' dyeing technique traditional to a small town in Calabria; we recovered a piece of Italian textile heritage that was about to be forgotten.

What would you like to see in the future of WRÅD? What are your objectives?
Our goal is simple: catalysing positive change. We have been pursuing this purpose through education and a programme we are right now strengthening for developing countries, through innovation and design (both of products and services). We want our brand to mean something – we developed WRÅD for a purpose higher than profits.

How can the circular economy play an important role in the process of creating a more sustainable and environmentally friendly fashion business?
Imagine the world as a box full of trash and human-made stuff. Imagine more people are projected to enter that box in the foreseeable future and all will be asking for more stuff. In order to survive we will have to figure out the way to make livable space by reusing what's already there! With textile production projected to increase by 67% by 2030 and 8 billion people walking a smaller and more exhausted planet everyday, the paradigmatic transition from a linear to a circular business model is mandatory.

How do you believe that circularity could become mainstream?
Two school of thoughts exist for the two types of people currently leading our companies: 1) For the LOHAS® leaders there is no question about it – circularity is the only way forward. More incentives and better legislation to create symbiotic relations among industries are needed to catalyse the efforts and aspirations of these leaders; 2) For the old-school capitalistic leaders, I suggest they take a look at the projected increase in the price of virgin raw materials in the next 10–15 years due to their increasing scarcity. Companies that do not invest in circular supply chains are likely to see a reduction in their EBIDTA [earnings before interest, taxes, depreciation and amortization] by 3–4%.

6.1.4 *The importance of collaborations for circularity*

Among Millennials and Gen Z, the presence of collaborations is a way to make products special and more appealing – unique even. In recent years there have been many successful collaborations between circular players and mainstreem brands/retailers/etailers. What follows is a synthetic presentation of some of them.

One the most important collaborations within the sportswear world is the one between Adidas and Parley, a partnership born from the desire to reduce the amount of plastic that reaches the oceans through collecting it and reusing it, thanks to continuous innovation, as recycled polyester. Adidas and Parley Ocean Plastic offers to their consumers a wide range of sportswear and running shoes. Any consumer interested in protecting the oceans can visit Parley's website, a platform that brings together a wide range of different artists, scientists and people from the STEAM disciplines: science, technology, engineering, art and mathematics. The idea is to 'put them all together to talk about the problem and bring them into the domains where the issue has not been talked about'.[20]

A real focus on sustainable topics can also be found in the luxury fashion world, through the work of brands like Salvatore Ferragamo – collaborating with Orange Fiber, Vivienne Westwood – collaborating with Progetto Quid, and producing 100% 'Made in Italy' headbands.

Also Stella McCartney implemented some partnerships that are helping the brand through the transition to a circular model, such as the collaboration with the Ellen MacArthur Foundation as well as the Cradle to Cradle Products Innovation Institute and a partnership with The RealReal (Box 19).

Another relevant collaboration is the one between Gucci and 'I was a Sari', featured in Gucci Equilibrium, the brand's programme and portal to connect people, planet and purpose. 'I was a Sari' is a social enterprise that perfectly encapsulates Gucci's drive toward social empowerment and commitment to the circular economy. The circular economy project led by Gucci involves the upcycling of left-over scrap leather and fabric materials to produce embroidery with one-off handcrafted designs. Women from marginalized communities in Mumbai are trained to become artisans and embroiderers to recreate saris from recycled ones, teaching them new skills and income to create futures for them and their families. "We can play an important role for a disruptive social and cultural change", states Rossella Ravagli, Head of Corporate Sustainability & Responsibility at Gucci.[21] Collaborations represent an important strategic tool also for WRÅD: one of the most recent and significant is the capsule collection done with

---

[20] Fabien Cousteau – https://www.parley.tv/#all-events.
[21] Source: www.equilibrium.gucci.com.

YOOX, one of the biggest online retailers, launched during the 10th anniversary of YOOXIGEN, Yoox's sustainability platform.

Celebrities are also getting more and more involved; a good example is the collaboration between EcoAlf – a sustainable fashion brand – and Gwyneth Paltrow, the famous actor, singer and businesswoman. The collaboration brought to fruition a vest and a backpack designed in collaboration with the famous actress.

Box 18 Progetto Quid

Founded in Verona in 2013, Quid has been providing stable and fair employment opportunities to those who struggle most to access the Italian job market through its own fashion brand, Progetto Quid – changing Italy's job market, one dress at a time. While enabling vulnerable individuals to redesign their future, Quid aims to redesign 'Made in Italy' fashion. Progetto Quid not only produces its own collections, using textile overstock, it also supplies established 'Made in Italy' partner brands with ethical collections. With a turnover of €2.8 million in 2018, five stores in northern Italy, a distribution network of over 100 multi-brand stores across the country, and eight continuing collaborations with brands like Calzedonia, Intimissimi and two majors national Fair-Trade chains, Quid is scaling up.

Quid was internationally recognized in 2017 with the Women for Results UN Momentum for Change Award, the EESC Civil Society Prize and the Angelo Ferro Prize for Social Innovation. In 2016 Quid was the only Italian project to be showcased at the Social Enterprise World Forum in Hong Kong, while in the 2015 it was a finalist in the Social Innovation Tournament (European Investment Bank Institute) and in 2014 won first prize at the European Social Innovation competition.

Since 2013 Quid has been offering fair and stable job opportunities to women struggling with disabilities, to prisoners and former inmates (employment rate below 30%), to recovering addicts (employment rate below 13%) as well as to other vulnerable groups. Quid employs both disadvantaged workers, for whom employment incentives apply,[22] and vulnerable workers[23] for whom no structured employment relief measures are in place yet. The latter include victims of human trafficking, victims of domestic violence, migrants, refugees and asylum seekers, NEETs (not in education, employment or training) and long-term unemployed individuals. Thanks to a network of over 12 local and national NGO partners, including Social Services, Comunità Papa Giovanni XXIII and Comunità di San Patrignano, Quid recruits those who strive for a new beginning. Today, across its own workshop, a

---

[22] Italian law ex L. 381/91.
[23] Italian law Dec. Min 07/2017.

workshop in Verona's prison and its stores, Quid employs 118 individuals – 90% of whom are women aged 19–65 and from 16 different countries, all of whom hold a share of the cooperative. They work across Quid's six units (production and packaging, logistics, finance and administration, style, sales, communications) while also acting as mentors and trainers for over 32 trainees and apprentices that Quid has welcomed since 2015. Through work these women not only become financially independent, but also grow in confidence and participate more in social life, overcoming barriers for themselves, their families and children.

This social mission is paired with an innovative, collaborative approach to the 'Made in Italy' ecosystem, with the aim to redesign it without sacrificing style.

Quid's creations are made from textile overstock – that is second-, but more often first-choice fabrics whose production has been discontinued. In 2018 Quid was able to prolong the lifecycle and maintain the value of over 300,000m of fabric thanks to a network of 20 textile manufacturers and brands who care about people and the environment – Zoli and Lisa to name just two.

Quid's own deadstock, in turn, is donated to a number of charitable projects from social entrepreneurship initiatives, with a focus on upcycling, organized by local schools in Verona to more structured social fashion projects such as Verona-based DHub and Centro Riuso Creativo, Recò in Iesi and Artesanos Don Bosco in Latin America.

Progetto Quid's collections, designed internally by Quid's Style Unit fill the niche for mid-range ethical fashion combining design and affordability and were chosen by 13,000 customers in 2017 alone. Progetto Quid also aims to influence established brands, championing an integrated and ethical approach to their supply chain. Since 2013 Quid has been the exclusive provider of ethical collections of accessories for a number of fashion and lifestyle brands. Today the company collaborates on a continuous basis with eight brands, including Calzedonia, Intimissimi, and Fair Trade and organic chains like AltroMercato and Naturasì. In autumn 2018 Quid collaborated with iconic brand Vivienne Westwood for a limited-edition 'Made in Italy' headband collection.

According to the social values of the Westwood company, Dame Vivienne has supported Progetto Quid in commissioning a headband collection. The bands are totaly handcrafted using iconic Westwood jacquard and silk fabrics.

Quid started collaborating with the Italian retailer Naturasì in 2016, creating co-branded collections of household accessories and the collaboration has since evolved, focusing on more innovative products. Meanwhile Burberry also initiated a partnership and started donating excess fabric to Progetto Quid.

Source: corporate material.

Box 19 Stella McCartney: materials and innovation

Stella McCartney, the fashion brand that carries the name of its founder (Stella Nina McCartney), is one of the industry's most vocal champions of environmental issues and a good example of the commercial potential of sustainable, ethically minded businesses. After a 17-year partnership with Kering, in 2018 both parties confirmed the split and the Fashion brand together with LVMH have reached an agreement to further develop the Stella McCartney House.[24] As stated in the press release, 'the goal of this partnership will be for the Stella McCartney House to accelerate its worldwide development in terms of business and strategy, while of course remaining faithful to its long-lasting commitment to sustainable and ethical luxury fashion'. (…) Bernard Arnault, Chairman and CEO of LVMH, declared: "I am extremely happy with this partnership with Stella. It is the beginning of a beautiful story together, and we are convinced of the great long-term potential of her House. A decisive factor was that she was the first to put sustainability and ethical issues on the front stage, very early on, and built her House around these issues."[25]

The official brand website has 3 sections dedicated to Sustainability: 'Mission statement', 'Materials and Innovation' and 'Reducing our impact' where it's easy to find information about Stella McCartney Environmentally friendly strategy.

Following a 360° approach to sustainability, Stella McCartney's stores and offices follow a Green Guidebook, updated each year that provides guidelines on how to save energy and water, ensure the waste is recycled, and reduce their overall environmental impact.[26]

As publicly stated, Stella McCartney is a no leather, no fur, no skins and no feathers brand. Moreover, none of their product are tested on animals, and the fragrances are not sold in China were government regulations require animal testing. Since 2008 all Stella McCartney products are PVC free and since 2013, following the PETA campaign, Angora free. PFCs cannot be used while producing a Stella McCartney product as well as cotton from Uzbekistan, Syria or Turkmenistan and viscose from ancient and endangered forests. None of the brand's denim has undergone the process of sandblasting and no wool is sourced from farms that allow mulesing. All of the wood, paper and packaging used is FSC-certified or from recycled sources.[27]

---

[24] Source: www.lvmh.it/notizie-documenti/comunicati-stampa/stella-mccartney-and-lvmh-announce-a-new-partnership-to-further-develop-the-stella-mccartney-house.

[25] Source: www.lvmh.it/notizie-documenti/comunicati-stampa/stella-mccartney-and-lvmh-announce-a-new-partnership-to-further-develop-the-stella-mccartney-house.

[26] Source: www.stellamccartney.com/experience/it/sustainability/our-stores-and-offices.

[27] Sources: www.stellamccartney.com/experience/it/sustainability/policies and https://www.stellamccartney.com/experience/it/sustainability/materials-and-innovation/fibres-from-forests.

> Stella McCartney strongly believes that the future of fashion is circular, restorative and regenerative in a way in which clothes we love never end up as waste. Some of the latest initiatives and partnership that are helping the brand through the transition to a circular model are: a collaboration with the Ellen MacArthur Foundation as well as the Cradle to Cradle Products Innovation Institute, a partnership with The RealReal – who provides the largest selection of pre-owned luxury items and the co-launch of Clevercare, which is a care symbol, a website and a communication campaign all rolled into one.[28]
> Stella McCartney's partners and collaborators are integral to helping the brand fulfil its mission. Some of the NGOs, brands and industry organisations that are working with Stella McCartney are: Adidas, Canopy, Coty, Kering, Kering Eyewear, Parley for the Oceans, Textile Exchange.[29]

References

Accenture-GCA (2018). Circular x Fashion Tech – Trend Report 2018.

Chouinard, Y. (2005). Let My People Go Surfing. 1st ed. New York: *Penguin Books*.

Circular Economy Strategy - Environment - European Commission (2019). [online] Available at: http://ec.europa.eu/environment/circular-economy/index_en.htm

Draper S., Murray V. and Weissbrod I. (2007). 'Fashioning Sustainability: A Review of the Sustainability Impacts on the Clothing Industry'. *London: Forum for the Future*.

Ellen MacArthur Foundation (2017). 'A New Textile Economy: Redesigning Fashion's Future'. Available at: http://www.ellenmacarthurfoundation.org/publications.

Euromonitor International (2016). 'The Global Circular Economy: The Impact of "Reduce, Re-use, Recycle" on Consumer Markets'. Available at: https://www.euromonitor.com/the-global-circular-economy-the-impact-of-reduce-re-use-recycle-on-consumer-markets/report.

European Commission (2019). 'Report from the Commission to the European Parliament, the Council, the European Economic and Social Committee and the Committee of the Regions' on the implementation of the Circular Economy Action Plan. Available at: https://eur-lex.europa.eu/legal-content/en/TXT/?uri=CELEX%3A52016DC0805.

---

[28] Source: www.stellamccartney.com/experience/it/sustainability/circularity-2.
[29] Source: www.stellamccartney.com/experience/it/sustainability/collaborations.

Fletcher, Kate. (2008). 'Sustainable Fashion and Clothing: Design Journeys'. London, Earthscan.

Global Fashion Agenda & Boston Consulting Group. (2018). 'The Pulse of the fashion industry 2018'. NY.

Global Fashion Agenda & The Boston Consulting Group. (2017). 'The Pulse of the fashion industry 2017'. NY.

Klanten, R. & Bohle, S. (2012). 'Cause and Effect: Visualizing Sustainability'. *Berlin, Gestalten.*

Korn W. (2012). 'Made on Earth: What We Wear. Where It Comes From. Where It Goes.' *London, Bloomsbury.*

McDonough, W. & Braungart, M. (2002). 'Cradle to Cradle: Remaking the Way We Make Things'. *New York: North Point Press.*

McDonough, W. & Braungart, M. (2013). 'The Upcycle'. *New York, North Point Press.*

McKinsey Global Institute (2011). 'Resource Revolution: Meeting the World's Energy, Materials, Food, and Water Needs'. Available at: https://www.mckinsey.com/business-functions/sustainability/our-insights/resource-revolution.

Minney, S. (2011). Naked Fashion: The New Sustainable Fashion Revolution. Oxford, New Internationalists.

Ricchetti, M. (2017). 'Neomateriali nell'economia circolare'. Moda. Milan, *Edizioni Ambiente.*

Rinaldi, F.R. & Testa S. (2014). 'The Responsible Fashion Company'. Abingdon, *Greenleaf Publishing/Routledge.*

7 Collaborative Consumption in Fashion

by *Francesca Romana Rinaldi*

> *The best collaborations create something bigger than the sum of what each person can create on their own.*
>
> Anonymous

Many companies have applied the logic of the sharing economy to fashion, initiating a phenomenon that has been defined as Collaborative Fashion Consumption (CFC). CFC has the potential to truly disrupt the fashion industry and establish itself as a new and validated consumption behaviour; it has the power to finally reconcile the long-standing dichotomy between fashion and sustainability, as it provides a solution to both the industry's environmental impact as well as to the need of consumers to keep up with trends. Having access to CFC platforms will enable people to reduce the number of clothes they buy while still satisfying their need for newness and the pursuit of the latest fashion trends. In this chapter the main business models of CFC (i.e. rental, subscription-rental and recommerce) will be presented and positive environmental effects of CFC will be discussed, together with the challenges of the main CFC business models.

7.1 Defining CFC

A formal definition of CFC has been provided by Iran and Schrader,[1] who assert that 'CFC embraces fashion consumption in which consumers, instead of buying new fashion products, have access to already existing garments either through alternative opportunities to acquire individual

---

[1] Iran and Schrader, 2017.

ownership (i.e. swapping or second hand) or through usage options for fashion products owned by others (i.e. renting or leasing)'.

While it is true that CFC activities are different and varied, they all fall under the definition of collaborative consumption as they entail the redistribution of used products, which are reused by two or more people regardless of whether ownership is shifted, or a monetary versus non-monetary compensation is envisaged.

These activities can either be based on a B2C or a P2P model. It is important to remark that most CFC activities are not new concepts. On the contrary, they have existed for a long time but, as they were traditionally applied locally within families or among friends and neighbours, their scope was intrinsically restrictive.

With the new opportunities offered by information and communication technologies, CFC activities have the potential to expand to unprecedented levels. The existence of an online platform, in fact, adds value to collaborative initiatives carried out in the traditional way as it promotes them to a broader scale while lowering transaction costs, allowing a wide variety of products to be shared easily and conveniently. For this reason, CFC has the potential to truly disrupt the fashion industry and establish itself as a new and validated consumption behaviour.

CFC has the power to finally reconcile the long-standing dichotomy between fashion and sustainability, as it provides a solution to both the industry's environmental impact as well as to the need of consumers to keep up with the trends: by participating in these initiatives, people will reduce the number of clothes they buy while still being able to satisfy their need for newness and the pursuit of the latest fashion trends.

The positive environmental effects of CFC will be discussed together with the limits to the diffusion of the CFC business models.

7.2   CFC main business models in practice[2]

According with Accenture and Fashion for Good in CFC there are three main business models that retailers and etailers can implement (see Box 20):

---

[2] Paragraph 7.2 is an extract from Accenture and Fashion for Good (2019), Box 20 is the result of an interview with Andrea Ruzzi, European fashion lead, Managing director at Accenture Italy & Europe, and Paola Sironi, fashion consultant at ACIN while the other boxes are the author's own elaboration.

- *Rental*: a one-off rental of a garment for a short time period, such as Rent the Runway;
- *Subscription-Rental*: a fee paid for access to a range of garments, such as MUD Jeans and Rent the Runway;
- *Recommerce*: the recovery and resale of a garment by the original retailer, such as Farfetch, Vestiaire Collective, Eileen Fisher and Patagonia.

Box 20 Accenture's point of view on collaborative consumption

As a global professional services company, Accenture is constantly looking ahead to anticipate what's coming next. Its Innovation Architecture uses an innovation-led approach to help clients develop and deliver disruptive innovations – and scale them faster. From research, ventures and labs to studios, innovation and delivery centers, Accenture helps companies imagine the future and then bring it to life.

At Accenture's innovation center in Milan (ACIN), which serves as the company's European hub for Fashion, the company leverages its global assets to address fundamental fashion industry challenges like sustainability.

In a 2019 report titled "The Future of Circular Fashion: Assessing the Viability of Circular Business Models,[3] Accenture Strategy in collaboration with Fashion for Good sought to understand the financial viability of three collaborative consumption business models: rental, subscription-rental and recommerce.

The report helps identify where collaborative consumption models are attractive today and some of the critical levers to enhance their future viability.

Using a bottom-up approach to calculate margin on a per-garment basis, each of these collaborative consumption business models was explored across 4 industry segments; the Value Market, Mid-Market, Premium and Luxury. The modeling logic and assumptions were validated by leading fashion retailers, circular innovators, and industry experts. Accenture also conducted interviews with 15 leading fashion retailers and innovators and undertook in-depth research to gain qualitative insights to support the financial modeling.

Circular business models will play an integral role in the sustainable transformation of the fashion industry which is being driven by the new consumer mindset in tandem with rapid innovation and the emergence of startups that will enable these models.

"If we don't do it, someone else will – or already is" VF Corp.

The time to act is now. The transition to collaborative consumption business models in the fashion industry has already begun. Adoption will progress and accelerate with or without the participation of large companies. Accenture's findings point

[3] Accenture Strategy and Fashion for Good, 2019.

to a positive business case that should encourage established retailers to embrace and implement circular models.
The findings are the following.

The financial viability varies by segment and by business model:

Rental
- *Rental is the Luxury option.* Rental should be profitable for incumbent Luxury retailers and should be explored in detail by industry leaders.
- *Premium and Mid-Market retailers should consider rental*, however financial viability depends on key strategic levers - Mid Market and Premium viability is contingent on rental price and number of turnovers.
- *Rental is unlikely to work in the Value Market.* The variable costs associated with the model, alongside quality limitations likely to reduce the total number of rentals, diminishes potential viability.

Subscription-Rental
- *Subscription can be financially viable across the Mid-Market, Premium and Luxury segments.*
- *Lower effective COGS (cost of goods sold)* can drive margin based on improved garment durability.
- *Churn (duration of subscription)*, number of exchanges and customer acquisition cost are key strategic considerations that impact viability.
- *Viability is dependent on customer offering and behavior.*

Recommerce
- *Recommerce is viable for a range of segments.* Recommerce could be profitable for incumbent retailers across the Mid-Market, Premium and Luxury segments.
- *Recommerce requires maturity and scale.* Recommerce models take time to kick off because of the need to obtain inventory and engage customers.
- *Recommerce price and inventory acquisition cost* are key strategic considerations that impact viability.
- *The operational simplicity of the model*, relative to others, drives further opportunity.

All three models explored can be financially viable for existing fashion retailers depending on the industry segment where they are implemented.
The best way to scale CFC strategies as a competitive asset is to deploy a combination of new business models and technologies to systemically reduce value erosion across the value chain and open the door to new opportunities for growth.
To sum up, our recommendations to fashion companies are the following:

- PRIORITIZE MODELS BASED ON MARKET SEGMENT: To be successful, retailers will need to prioritize the CFC models with the highest potential for their industry segment.

- MATCH THE BUSINESS MODEL TO THE PRODUCT: Different product types are best suited to particular business models.
  - Rental: Products used infrequently, used for one-off events, or used for specific activities.
  - Subscription Rental: Products that customers regularly purchase.
  - Recommerce: Products that are high quality and durable.
- GET THE INCENTIVES RIGHT: These models all require a fundamental shift in customer behaviors to achieve scale.
  - Incentivize customers to act differently (i.e. encourage vouchers for Recommerce.
  - Ensure the customer experience is frictionless and sustainable (from garment collection to delivery). All the new activities required to make these models work (e.g. laundry, logistics) should be designed to optimize sustainability (e.g. chemical-free cleaning with companies such as Tersus, or electric vehicles for last-mile delivery etc.).

7.2.1 *Rental business model*

The rental business model is a one-off rental of a garment for a short time period, such as Rent the Runway (see Box 21). Rental in fashion is not new. It has been part of the industry for decades, especially in the special occasion segment. Today, it is transforming from a dated model to an innovative, modern way of consuming fashion.[4]

Factors that are accelerating this disruption include:

- *Recognition of wasted capacity*: there is a sharper focus than ever on the value of wasted capacity in fashion; about 50% of items in a customer's wardrobe are unworn,[5] creating an estimated $30bn worth of unworn items in UK wardrobes alone.[6]
- *Demand for access over ownership*: customers are demanding newness, variety and access in fashion. Rental can cater to these de-

---

[4] The Guardian, 2017.
[5] Fashion United, 2018.
[6] WARP, 2017.

mands in a less environmentally damaging way than the existing model. Furthermore, the same customers are increasingly demanding retailers to have a position on sustainability – 73% of millennial customers would shift to a brand with a clear purpose[7] – and those aligning proactively can capture market share.

- *Customer value*: the key driver for rental is its ability to offer a customer-centric, affordable solution for a rare occasion that may otherwise be too expensive. Rental allows customers to wear previously unaffordable and unattainable garments.

The fashion rental market is projected to be worth $1.9bn globally by 2023 – doubling in value from 2017.[8] Given, this market potential, certain important aspects must be considered.

Rental viability is influenced by a number of key factors. Specifically, Accenture's research found that the *rental price* and the number of *rentals per year* are both critical levers that alone can hugely influence the viability of the rental model. This represents a challenge for the value segment in all scenarios and fundamentals need to change, for instance, the durability of items for the industry as a whole would need to be prolonged. Accenture's assumptions would indicate that Luxury is highly viable, and that the Mid-Market and Premium segments are perhaps the most promising.

The key numbers in synthesis are the following:

- *Mid-Market segment*: the margin is positive after >15 rentals, charging a rental fee of >20% of the retail price.
- *Premium segment*: the margin is positive after >10 rentals, charging a rental fee of >20% of the retail price.
- *Luxury segment*: the margin is positive after >5 rentals, charging a rental fee of >5% of the retail price.

Uptake of Rental remains limited, but the opportunity is clear: research found that 50% of millennials would like to use rental fashion models.[9]

Benefits for the environment would include reduced demand for materials. Rental could play a transformative role in moving the industry toward a

---

[7] Nielsen, 2015.
[8] Reuters, 2018.
[9] Harpers Bazaar, 2018.

less resource-intensive model by incentivizing higher production standards and greater garment longevity. The purchase displacement rate must be considered a key metric when assessing potential environmental benefits.

Box 21 Rent the Runway

Rent the Runway (RTR) is a rental and subscription-rental fashion platform founded in 2009 by two Harvard Business School graduates – Jennifer Hyman and Jennifer Fleiss.

Access is free and users can choose to rent from a wide range of clothes suited to different events, and for a limited period of time users can choose from different designers' best products related to suggested categories.

For the "one-time" rental, users have two different options: a 4-day or an 8-day rental. For the "renting with membership" option, called "RTR unlimited" members can have 4+ items shipped at home at a time and swap them for something new whenever they want and have access to membership-only discounts to buy the items they want to keep.

At the end of their rental period, the customer is required to either drop off the items at the nearest UPS facility or RTR store, or, schedule a UPS pickup.[10]

Source: author's adaptation from www.renttherunway.com.

7.2.2   *Subscription-rental business model*

Revenues in the "subscription-rental" business model come from customer fees paid to access a range of garments plus any additional income from customer purchases.[11]

Examples are Rent the Runway (see Box 21) and MUD Jeans (see Box 22).

Subscription models in fashion have grown >100% in 5 years, driven by demand from young, high-earning urban consumers,[12] with companies capitalizing on low barriers to entry. Fashion currently represents about 6% of the global subscription market and is rapidly expanding.[13]

---

[10] www.renttherunway.com, 2019.

[11] More broadly, Accenture's research identified three distinct approaches to subscription model: subscription box services (such as Stitch Fix), subscription-rental (such as Rent the Runway) and closed-loop subscription (such as For days).

[12] Forbes, 2018b.

[13] Hackernoon, 2018.

Subscription models have now been adopted across a range of geographies and segments at reasonable scale. The increasing trend toward subscription in fashion is predominately driven by consumers who value access over ownership, especially when it gives them a wider variety of options in casualwear. Subscription fashion models therefore enable consumers to try new items and to experiment with minimal risk.

Subscription-rental marketplace leaders are focused on providing customer-centric solutions for fashion – a wardrobe on demand, flexibility and service. As part of the deal, most leaders offer unlimited exchanges on a set number of garments.

Accenture's research[14] found that, while customer-centric, the *number of customer exchanges* (calculated based on assumptions of churn and frequency of turnaround) can have a huge influence on the financial viability of business models. Individual customer behavior has now become a critical factor in determining viability.

There is still relative uncertainty about the usage of these services given their very recent emergence and this of course is a critical consideration for retailers. In striving to balance value with costs, successful retailers will seek to encourage low refresh rates whilst retaining the impression of generous flexibility.

The key numbers in a nutshell are the following:

- *In the Mid-Market*: more than 15 exchanges per subscription would bring the margin below the current baseline;[15] at more than 25 garment exchanges – which would happen if a customer exchanged a garment every about 5 weeks – the model would lose money.
- *In the Premium Market*: the equivalent rate of exchange is only slightly higher, i.e. 17 for margin lower than the baseline and 28 to generate a negative margin.

Driving this high sensitivity are the new variable costs, including postage, packaging, laundry and manpower, which are incurred for every exchange with no additional revenue uplift. The challenge is to ensure a balance

---

[14] Accenture Strategy and Fashion for Good, 2019.
[15] The baseline is the guideline margin across each of the four industry segments and it was calculated based on publicly available financial data, with the margin percentages verified by retailers during interviews.

7 Collaborative Consumption in Fashion

between offering convenient, customer-centric models while optimizing associated costs.

Benefits for the environment could be the savings in materials. The environmental impact of subscription-rental is largely dependent on the purchase displacement rate. This will be especially important as subscription-rental is scaled up, with a potential risk that overall consumption could increase if uptake of the model takes place alongside traditional linear fashion. If the new models are supplementary to existing consumer purchasing this will increase volumes of production and waste.

Box 22 MUD Jeans

Company information

- HQ in Almere, The Netherlands
- Founded in 2012 by Bert van Son
- Seven staff members
- Work with three factories, two for fabrics and one for stitching and washing
- Turnover (2017) – €822,000 (75% sales: 25% lease)
- Partnership with RE: Pack a returnable packaging company[16]

MUD jeans are made from 40% recycled content, the material being derived from discarded jeans. The jeans are offered on a CFC subscription-rental model, so that repairs are free and users can swap their jeans for a new pair.

MUD Jeans is a Dutch premium jeanswear brand that started in 2012, when Bert van Son founded the company. His 30 years' experience in the fashion industry made him realize how dirty and unfair the industry is most of the time. He has witnessed that life for factory workers is extremely demanding, and that it makes great demands of nature. He therefore decided this was something he wanted to change.

Bert believes that having fun without destroying the earth and its resources is possible. As an amateur sailor he realizes how strong nature is and how the elements master you. Together with his team, Bert transformed MUD Jeans into an exemplary company, consistently putting circular economy principles into practice. He is mastering the fashion industry on a different level.

MUD Jeans aims to make good-quality, ethical jeans available to more people. Our jeans already tick about every box on the ethical checklist, but then we took it a step further. In 2013, MUD Jeans launched the pioneering lease system. This

---

[16] Source: www.ellenmacarthurfoundation.org

system ensures that we keep hold of our valuable fibres and that every garment comes back to us and gets recycled. Repairs are provided for free and the customers can keep the jeans for as long as they want, with a repair service provided for free. Or they can swap them for a new pair after the one-year rental term is complete. It resulted in global media awareness and Bert sharing the MUD Jeans story worldwide.

How was the idea of MUD born and how did it evolve?
MUD Jeans originates from the belief that there should be an alternative to fast fashion. Team MUD wants to radically change the fashion industry, starting with the most popular clothing item, a pair of jeans. In 2013 MUD Jeans introduced 'Lease A Jeans', an innovative way of guilt-free consumption, allowing consumers to shop consciously, do good for the environment and look fashionable.

What is the 'MUD Method'?
The MUD method is our methodology for a better fashion industry and consists of nine concepts. The Circular Economy, Fair Fashion, Zero-Impact Jeans, Premium Quality, Repair Service, Upcycled Jeans, Organic & Vegan, Send Old Jeans & Lease A Jeans.

Circular Economy
By being part of the Circular Economy, we are creating a world where there is no such thing as waste. At the moment, our jeans contain between 23% and 40% post-consumer recycled denim.

Fair Fashion
We learned that if something is surprisingly cheap, someone else, somewhere in the world, is paying for it. That's why we keep our supply chain short and see our suppliers as our friends rather than business acquaintances. We are proud to say the denim experts in the factories sew and stitch with a smile on their faces and earn above minimum wage.

Zero-Impact Jeans
We said goodbye to the old and dirty techniques. We eliminated PP spray, use Cradle2Cradle (C2C) indigo dye and our factory's laundry recycles 95% of its water through reverse osmosis.

Premium Quality
Our styles are made to last and are trans-seasonal. This means that we do not have collections, which most importantly allows us to save resources.

Repair Service
We want our customers to wear their MUD Jeans as long as possible. For the members of our MUD community we offer free repairs during their leasing period.

Upcycled Jeans
We believe that good-quality, pre-loved MUD Jeans deserve a second chance. That is why we sell used MUD Jeans through our Vintage Programme.

Organic & Vegan
At MUD Jeans we have a holistic approach to caring. That's why our jeans consist of recycled and organic cotton and we use printed labels instead of leather patches.

Send Old Jeans
We take back pre-loved denim, whatever brand they are from. They just need to be made of 96% cotton or more. New customers get €10 off their purchase or a month's free lease and we'll recycle them into new, cool denim.

Lease A Jeans
MUD Jeans introduced a pioneering Lease A Jeans model. This innovative approach aims to prevent overconsumption. Consumers can 'rent' the jeans and return them to us after a year of use. This way we ensure we stay the owners of the raw material and get them back at the end of life.

Source: https://mudjeans.eu; Interview with Eva Engelen, CSR responsible at MUD Jeans.

7.2.3 Recommerce business model

The recommerce business model is based on the recovery and resale of a garment by the original retailer. Examples include Eileen Fisher (see Box 23), Vestiaire Collective, Patagonia, Farfetch, and The RealReal.

Revenue is generated in this case by a one-off fee paid that the new customer pays to the retailer to purchase a previously-owned garment, where the retailer has acquired the garment back from the original owner.

Recommerce – the resale of previously sold items – is well-established in fashion. Historically, it has tended to be somewhat informal and was spearheaded by charity shops, flea-markets and second-hand sales. Today, it is securing a foothold as a formal part of the industry and is growing. A recent report showed that resale has grown 21 times faster than traditional retail over the past three years.[17]

---

[17] ThredUp, 2019.

This has driven innovation at scale, with early adopters seeking to establish a share of a formalized recommerce market.

This growth is driven by:

- *Changing perception of used clothes*: the perception of previously owned garments has changed; used garments are no longer seen as dirty and outdated but instead customers place value on second-hand, vintage products.[18]
- *Customer value proposition*: recommerce drives value for the original owner (who receives a return on the investment through returning the garment, either through cash or a voucher incentive) and the new buyer (who purchases a garment at a reduced price and can therefore afford a higher-quality garment, perhaps from a retailer previously out of budget).
- *Reducing process friction*: advances in technology have made recommerce easier. Further help has come from optimized collections, enhanced merchandising and curation platforms, and through scale that further incentivize participation.

Recommerce is the most mature CFC business model today. By 2023, the market is set to reach $51bn, with annual growth of 16%.[19]

Growth has been driven by improved access to marketplaces for second-hand garments, with tech-led solutions such as Depop emerging with a specific focus on millennial consumers. Marketplaces have also emerged for specific segments and products.[20]

Recommerce is generally a very viable model – however, a major challenge for incumbent retailers is how to get the garments / products back from existing customers to build up inventory.

This is a particularly big challenge given the wide variety of options available for customers to return items – with high-value opportunities through a growing number of independent marketplaces. While customer value and convenience are both critical considerations when designing a model that is likely to target customers based on convenience above other metrics, the reality is that the financial incentive for return is still critical.

---

[18] ThredUp, 2018.
[19] ThredUp, 2019.
[20] Forbes, 2018a.

One element in this is the discount voucher incentive that is offered to customers returning items: in each case, this erodes margin.

An interesting challenge is to be found in the higher value segments, where there may be a need to offer bigger voucher incentives given the higher value of the item.

More detailed consumer insight is needed in order to better understand the key drivers, motivators and channels behind recommerce, and to build a clear vision of the full spectrum from convenience to reward.

The dominance of independent platforms and startups creates a risk for established retailers in terms of garment authentication and quality. At the same time, brands miss out on the potential benefits of owning these channels – as well as the additional revenue streams, deeper customer relationships and new customer touch points that they inevitably generate. Many innovative leaders such as Farfetch are now responding to this risk and have already incorporated recommerce into their existing business.

Examples of recommerce are often cited as a collaboration between start-ups and established retailers. Leading initiatives include Worn Wear, a collaboration between Patagonia and Yerdle, in which post-consumer garments are returned and resold; and The North Face Renewed, a collaboration between The North Face and The Renewal Workshop, focused on selling pre-consumer, defective or unsold stock that is refurbished and resold.

Summarizing, the key numbers are as follows:[21]

- The price at which the garment is listed for resale relative to the original retail price, ranges from 25% to 65%. Exactly where retailers choose to position themselves on this spectrum is critical for determining financial viability, particularly in the Mid-Market and Premium segments.
- In the Mid-Market, the price charged would need to be more than 35% of the original retail price for the model to be profitable.
- The Premium Market is a little less price sensitive and should remain profitable with garment prices set at below 30% of the original retail price.

---

[21] Accenture Strategy and Fashion for Good, 2019.

- Luxury produces positive margins below 10% of the original retail price, demonstrating that luxury retailers have an opportunity to offer very steep discounts on resale.

This should make it possible to engage new customers at lower price points and improve the viability of recommerce. However, while there is a saturated market for independent players in Luxury, Accenture's interviews identified some of the uncertainties that make retailers cautious. These include the impacts on perceived value of new goods and on the brand overall, changes in customer demand for new items and on the possible cannibalization of existing retail channels. Each of these would need to be carefully managed and explored further. A go-to market strategy would be contingent upon conducting deeper customer research.

Benefits for the environment flow from re-use of materials. This model has clear environmental value: re-use extends the lifecycle of a garment by an average of 2.2 years, potentially reducing its water / carbon / waste footprint by up to 73%.[22] If adopted at scale, recommerce could potentially shift customers' understanding of how garments can retain value beyond the point of sale and discourage the perception that they are disposable.

Box 23 Eileen Fisher's three lives of a product

Eileen Fisher Inc. makes practical and 'sophisticated suburban' women's clothing, specializing in loose-fitting timeless garments that are updated only slightly from year to year. Eileen Fisher started her eponymous company in 1984, when she had a basic idea: that women wanted chic, simple clothes that made getting dressed easy. With the modular line, pieces can be mixed and matched from season to season, providing the unique selling proposition.

Today the company comprises 1,100 people with more than 60 stores in the United States, Canada and the United Kingdom.[23] Fisher lives in Irvington, New York, where the company is headquartered. In 2005, she sold the $300 million company to her 875 employees through an employee stock ownership plan, or ESOP. She is now the co-CEO. Fisher is ethically product oriented, with a focus on reducing environmental impact and boosting Fair Trade practices for workers around the world. The company is constantly adjusting its supply chain, from dyes to transpor-

---

[22] Circle Economy, 2019.
[23] Fisher, 2019.

tation to farming, in an effort to contribute to a better future for the planet.[24] The company produced its first organic cotton product in 2004. Today, 98% of the cotton in Fisher's current collections are made from organic cotton, and the company is moving toward making more of its clothes with non-toxic dyeing practices.[25] Eileen Fisher's website describes the three lives of a product:

- 'First Life' of clothes that are made to last. 'We design simple, timeless clothes in the most sustainable fabrics.'
- 'Second Life': 'when you no longer wear your clothes, we take them back'. Pieces still in perfect condition are given a good-as-new cleaning and resold through Eileen Fisher's Renew program.[26] The brand's philosophy is simple: buy quality pieces, wear them as long as possible, and when you're done with them, pass them on to someone else.
- 'Third Life': for pieces taken back that are damaged beyond repair. 'Eileen Fisher's Waste No More team transforms them into one-of-a-kind artworks, pillows and wall hangings using a custom felting method.'

In 2009, Eileen Fisher started a take-back programme – part of a circular system designed to preserve the value of our clothes at every stage, in any condition. They have collected, up to 2019, over 1.2 million garments since then. It's an ambitious experiment, rooted in a deep appreciation for the value of renewable materials – one that takes an artisanal approach to craft and technology.[27]

7.3 How can consumers benefit from CFC?

In addition to ecological effects, CFC also offers many advantages to consumers.

As previously mentioned, fashion rental and subscription-rental services have the primary benefit of offering people a greater variety of choices, enabling them to continuously update their wardrobe and keep up with fashion trends without spending exorbitant amounts of money.[28]

Moreover, the absence of ownership commitment relieves people from the fear of making mistake purchases, allowing them to freely and cre-

---

[24] CNN, Available at: https://us.cnn.com/2019/02/22/cnn-underscored/eileen-fisher-clothing-sale-2019/index.html.
[25] Close, 2019.
[26] https://www.eileenfisherrenew.com.
[27] https://www.wastenomore.com.
[28] Pike, 2016.

atively experiment with new styles and items and express their individuality.[29]

Finally, CFC services provide access to expensive designer labels, hence becoming particularly appealing to aspirational consumers who could normally not afford them.[30]

For recommerce or clothes-swapping, money savings constitute a driver not only for consumers with limited financial possibilities but also to those who want to cut their spending on clothes, regardless of their income levels. Ceding fashion items, on the other hand, would alleviate the feelings of guilt arising from purchasing items that were rarely worn.[31] These types of CFC also allow the possibility to obtain unique and rare items that are not mass produced.[32] Botsman and Rogers[33] also mention the emotional gratification that people who give up unwanted fashion items experience when they see them leave with satisfied new owners.

Finally, ethical and environmental motives represent a driver to engage in CFC;[34] therefore, when practicing CFC people might feel gratified by their direct contribution to a more sustainable consumption.[35]

7.4 Inhibitors to CFC from the consumer's point of view

While CFC has the promising potential to contribute to a more sustainable society, it is not exempt from limitations.

First of all, the ecological effect is uncertain and it varies depending on the specific scenario.[36] In investigating the possible environmental impact of CFC, several studies have highlighted potential rebound effects that might offset the environmental gains. The results of some studies[37] confirmed the potential positive ecological effects of CFC, provided that the garments' service lives are considerably extended. However, they also

---

[29] Pedersen and Netter, 2015.
[30] Pedersen and Netter, 2015; Pike, 2016.
[31] Joung, 2014.
[32] Becker-Leifhold and Iran, 2018.
[33] Botsman and Rogers, 2010.
[34] Becker-Leifhold and Iran, 2018.
[35] Pedersen and Netter, 2015.
[36] Iran and Schrader, 2017.
[37] Zamani *et al.*, 2017.

highlighted the risk of offsetting benefits as a result of increased goods transactions costs: since clothes are passed to many other peers and companies instead of staying in the same household for their whole lifecycle, additional transportation is necessary, which in turn increases CO_2 emissions. Therefore, logistical aspects must be carefully analysed when implementing CFC business models.

Ecological effects might also be counterbalanced by the extra effort in garment care that is needed in CFC, as each item will be treated in such a way as to make it look 'as new'. While it is true that professional garment care is more ecological than private care due to resource saving, it is also true that the number of washes would greatly increase under CFC. In fact, while private owners would not generally wash certain items, such as coats, after a single use, rental companies must always do so for hygiene reasons as clothes are passed on to other people.[38]

Secondly, CFC might actually increase the number of products used instead of producing sufficiency effects.[39] This is mainly due to two reasons: on the one hand, as all types of CFC allow for a cheaper consumption of clothes, the demand for fashion items would increase. This is especially true in the case of rental services of designer brands, which, thanks to CFC models, will become an option even to those who could not normally afford them; these consumers therefore represent extra consumption compared to a scenario without CFC.[40] On the other hand, in order to be appealing, the offer of CFC initiatives should be wide and varied, hence requiring additional products.

Thirdly, the environmental effects will occur only if CFC actually substitutes the purchase of new clothes rather than just being parallel to it. However, as long as fast fashion products will keep having such absurdly low prices, it is unlikely that consumers will stop buying them, especially considering the much higher price one would have to pay to rent a designer dress for just a limited time period.[41]

Finally, the concept of critical mass shall be considered. This refers to 'the existence of enough momentum in a system to make it become

---

[38] Iran and Schrader, 2017.
[39] Iran and Schrader, 2017.
[40] Iran and Schrader, 2017.
[41] Iran and Schrader, 2017.

self-sustaining',[42] which is vital for collaborative consumption, both in general and in fashion. In fact, in order to compete with traditional shopping, collaborative consumption should offer enough choices to be able to satisfy consumers. In CFC, this is especially true if we consider second-hand and swapping initiatives, which, to be attractive in the eye of consumers, should offer enough items so that everyone could find something they like.

The second reason why critical mass is so important in collaborative consumption is that it serves the function of 'social proof'. This means that once a certain number of early adopters is achieved, others will be convinced that those initiatives are something worthy of trying. This is because most individuals decide what to do based on what others are doing, and therefore need to see a critical mass of consumers implement a certain behaviour before adopting it themselves. In other words, critical mass allows to demolish the psychological barrier that often hinders new consumption patterns.[43]

Unfortunately, at the moment CFC still represents a niche market and it is far from achieving such critical mass.[44] This is mainly due to the existence of consumers' adoption barriers that challenge the spread of CFC.[45] First of all, the main issues arise from health and hygiene concerns, as consumers worry about the cleanliness of used clothes and fear the contact of previous owners' bacteria as well as the transmission of diseases. Secondly, CFC requires an important behavioural shift in consumption, as consumers might not feel as comfortable in sharing their clothes as they are in sharing cars or accommodation.[46] Moreover, people might be hindered from adopting CFC practices as these do not induce the same emotional high that derives from impulse purchase.[47] Finally, while it is true that the fracture of ownership is pervading most aspects of our everyday lives, there might still be considerable barriers in breaking this material bond with clothing. According to Belk,[48] individuals regard their possessions as part of themselves and they use them to construct their identity;

---

[42] Botsman and Rogers, 2010, p. 75.
[43] Botsman and Rogers, 2010.
[44] Iran and Schrader, 2017.
[45] Becker-Leifhold and Iran, 2018.
[46] Pike, 2016.
[47] Becker-Leifhold and Iran, 2018.
[48] According to Belk, 1988.

therefore, these greatly contribute to build and reflect their image. Clothes represent the first layer of the extended self,[49] as people use them as a tool of self-presentation.[50] Several studies have in fact shown that individuals identify themselves and others through clothing, which they effectively perceive as a representation of the self.[51] For this reason, giving up ownership of clothing might be more difficult compared to other items, and, as a consequence, the spread of CFC might be hindered.

References

Accenture Strategy and Fashion for Good (2019), 'The Future of Circular Fashion: Assessing the Viability of Circular Business Models'. Available at: https://fashionforgood.com/our_news/driving-circular-business-models-in-fashion/.

Alliedmarketresearch.com (2019). 'Online Clothing Rental Market by End-Users (Women, Men and Kids) and Clothing Style (Ethnic, Western and Others) – Global Opportunity Analysis And Industry Forecast, 2017–2023'. Official website of Allied Market Research. Available at: https://www.alliedmarketresearch.com/online-clothing-rental-market.

Becker-Leifhold, C. & Iran, S. (2018). 'Collaborative fashion consumption – drivers, barriers and future pathways'. *Journal of Fashion Marketing and Management: An International Journal*, 22(2), 189–208.

Belk, R.W. (1988). 'Possessions and the extended self'. *Journal of Consumer Research*, 15(2), 139–168.

BoF (2019). 'Rent the Runway Aims to Be "Amazon Prime of Rental"'. Available at: https://www.businessoffashion.com/articles/news-analysis/rent-the-runway-aims-to-be-amazon-prime-of-rental.

Botsman, R. & Rogers, R., (2010). *What's Mine Is Yours*. London: Harper Collins.

Carson, B. (2016). 'Rent The Runway, the "Netflix for dresses", just raised another $60 million and claimed profitability for the first time'. *Business Insider*. Available at: https://www.businessinsider.com/rent-the-runway-profitable-raises-60-million-fidelity-2016-12?IR=T.

Circle Economy (2019), The Circular Activation Project (http://new.circle-economy-com/switching-gear).

Close, K. (2019). 'Fashion Designer Eileen Fisher's $210 Million Fortune Built On Simple Basics'. *Forbes*, Available at: https://www.forbes.com/sites/kerry-

---

[49] Iran and Schrader, 2017.
[50] McNeill, 2018.
[51] McNeill, 2018.

close/2015/05/28/fashion-designer-eileen-fishers-210-million-fortune-built-on-simple-basics/#68dd0d2879ef.

Eisenmann, T. R. & Winig, L. (2012). 'Rent the Runway'. Harvard Business School. Available at: https://www.hbs.edu/faculty/Pages/item.aspx?num=41142.

Fashion United (2018). 'People do not wear at least 50 percent of their wardrobes, says study'. Available: https://fashionunited.uk/news/fashion/people-do-not-wear-at-least-50-percent-of-their-wardrobes-according-to-study/20180 81638356.

Fisher, E. (2019). 'Meet Eileen Fisher'. Available at: https://www.eileenfisher.com/meet-eileen/meet-eileen/?___store=en&___from_store=default.

Forbes (2018a). 'The Profitable Hidden Sneaker Market'. Available at: https://www.forbes.com/sites/leighsteinberg/2018/09/17/the-profitable-hidden-sneaker-market/#28f6bdd05925.

Forbes (2018b). 'The State of the Subscription Economy'. Available at: https://www.forbes.com/sites/louiscolumbus/2018/03/04/the-state-of-the-subscription-economy-2018/#5939e86e53ef.

The Guardian (2017). 'Spotify for fashion: does renting clothes signal the end for our wardrobes?'. Available at: https://www.theguardian.com/fashion/2017/nov/01/spotify-for-fashion-renting-clothes-walk-in-closet-obsolete-rental-subscription-brands-dior-prada.

Hackernoon (2018). 'How big is the global subscription box industry?' Available at: https://hackernoon.com/how-big-is-the-globalsubscription-box-industry-4b8dcb756937.

Harpers Bazaar (2018). 'Could rental fashion help us become more sustainable?' Available at: https://www.harpersbazaar.com/uk/fashion/fashion-news/a22 611439/rental-fashion-help-us-become-more-sustainable/.

Iran, S. & Schrader, U. (2017). 'Collaborative fashion consumption and its environmental effects'. *Journal of Fashion Marketing and Management*, 21(4), 468–482.

Joung, H. (2014). 'Fast-fashion consumers' post-purchase behaviours'. *International Journal of Retail & Distribution Management*, 42(8), 688–697.

McNeill, L. S. (2018). 'Fashion and women's self-concept: a typology for self-fashioning using clothing'. *Journal of Fashion Marketing and Management*, 22(1), 82–98.

New York Times (2019). 'Rent the Runway now valued at $1 billion with new funding'. Available at: https://www.nytimes.com/2019/03/21/business/rent-the-runway-unicorn.html.

Nielsen (2015). 'Global Corporate Sustainability Report'. Available at: https://engageforgood.com/2015-nielsen-global-sustainability-report/.

Pedersen, E. R. G. & Netter, S. (2015). 'Collaborative consumption: business model opportunities and barriers for fashion libraries'. *Journal of Fashion Marketing and Management*, 19(3), 258–273.

Pike, H. (2016). The Business of Fashion. Available at: https://www.businessoffashion.com/articles/fashion-tech/will-the-sharing-economy-work-for-fashion-rent-the-runway-rental.

Reuters (2018). 'The global online clothing rental market is expected to showcase a significant CAGR of 10% during the forecast period 2015–2023'. Available at: https://www.reuters.com/brandfeatures/venture-capital/article?id=44966.

ThredUp (2018). '2018 Resale Report'.

ThredUp (2019). 'ThredUp 2019 Resale Report'. Available at: https://www.thredup.com/resale.

WRAP (2017). 'Valuing Our Clothes'. Available at: http://www.wrap.org.uk/sites/files/wrap/valuing-our-clothes-the-cost-of-uk-fashion_WRAP.pdf.

Zamani, B., Sandin, G. & Peters, G. M. (2017). 'Life cycle assessment of clothing libraries: can collaborative consumption reduce the environmental impact of fast fashion?' *Journal of Cleaner Production*, 162, 1368–1375.

8 The Purpose of Business, B-Corps and Benefit Corporations

by *Paolo Di Cesare, Eric Ezechieli, Samira Tasso, Silvia Zanazzi, Nicola Piccolo and Letizia Rigazzi*

This chapter is focused on the very purpose of business and on the opportunities that the Certified B Corp and Benefit Corporation model have created in the fashion industry. The key concepts will be explained and supported by a best-practices discussion that will show in practice the opportunities of becoming a Certified B Corp.

A preliminary description of the B Corp certification and of the Benefit Corporation legal form will present the evolution of the business-as-usual approach towards a double-purpose model that maximizes both the positive impact and the profit created by a company, and will deepen how these approaches are changing the way companies face the challenges and opportunities of the contemporary context.

The case studies will then provide the reader with concrete examples of how some key players in the fashion industry have developed effective and innovative ways of incorporating the sustainability principles in their everyday business practices. The adoption of the B Corp model turns out to be the driver that enables businesses to become a force for good.

8.1 The shareholders paradigm

Business is a technology invented by man and, as such, it operates according to its rules. So far, the main rule applied has been based on an extremely simple equation: top managers are elected by shareholders and they receive full authority to manage the business; this authority is subject to the sole purpose for which the company is created, that is, to create a financial return for shareholders according to fiduciary and loyalty obligations (the so-called 'shareholder primacy' paradigm). Stakeholders, society and the environment are not contemplated within this system.

What would happen if the equation underlying business also considered all the other stakeholders, and included the measurement of the benefit caused to them with the same rigour that characterizes the measurement of shareholders' returns? A few years ago, some American entrepreneurs began to answer this question with the ultimate aim of making an evolutionary leap to the most powerful technology we managed to create so far: business.

8.2 B Corp & Benefit Corporation: the regenerative paradigm

Benefit Corporations are companies with a dual purpose, and will reach better economic results compared to competitors.
Robert Shiller, winner of the Nobel Prize for Economics, 2013

B certification and/or incorporation gives us the common tools we need to assess the positive and negative impacts of our practices, make and measure improvements, and share what we learn.
Vincent Stanley, Director of Philosophy, Patagonia

A Benefit Corporation is an incorporating structure similar to a For Profit Company, sole proprietorship, partnership or LLC. Unlike these other entities, however, a Benefit Corporation must consider the impact of its business decisions on all stakeholders, not just shareholders or members, but also society and the environment, to create a material positive impact on all of them.

B Corps are for-profit companies that together form a global movement within which they transform themselves from reality to a single purpose (profit) into organisms with two purposes: profit and positive impact on society and the environment. The vision that represents these principles is to use business as a positive force to create lasting and shared prosperity.

The B Corp movement was born in 2006 in the USA when some entrepreneurs decided that it was essential to try to change the dominant model and to promote a radical evolution of capitalism as we know it today. B Corp certification is the functional equivalent of Rainforest Alliance, LEED or Fair Trade labels. To become certified, a company must apply to B Lab, a specific non-profit organization that created the B Corp Certification and promotes the Benefit Corporation legal form globally. B Lab independently evaluates all applicant companies through the B Impact Assessment (BIA).[1]

The BIA (Figures 16 and 17) is an online analysis tool, and it has already been adopted by more than 100,000 companies that represent 150 sectors in 60 countries.[2]

Figure 16 BIA score distribution

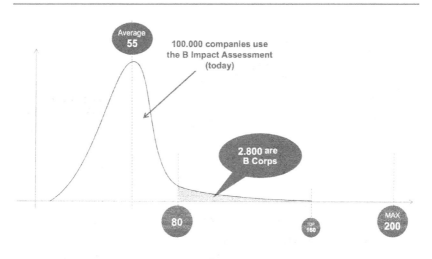

Source: B Lab, graphic elaboration by Nativa.

The tool provides information on the economic, social and environmental performance of the company, taking into account five macro areas of analysis: governance, community, people, environment and business model. The analysis results in the company obtaining a numerical score between 0 and 200 points, representing the impact caused by the company, its impact profile and areas of possible improvement. After the analysis has been certified through appraisal by the B Lab Review team, companies that exceed the score of 80/200, are recognized as Certified B Corp®.[3]

---

[1] https://bcorporation.net
[2] Bianchi and Fasan, 2017.
[3] Bianchi and Fasan, 2017.

Figure 17 The difference between extractive and regenerative[4] companies according to the BIA.

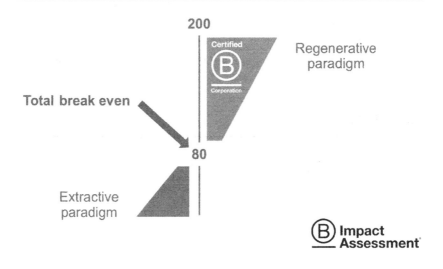

Source: B Lab, graphic elaboration by Nativa.

Only companies with a score of 80 or higher are eligible. Once approved, they must recertify every three years.

A company does not need to be a Benefit Corporation to become a Certified B Corp., although you may need to become a Benefit Corporation to remain a Certified B Corp. In addition to the BIA measuring tool, since 2008 B Lab has promoted the adoption of an ad hoc legal form which recognizes and guarantees the dual purpose of regenerative companies: the Benefit Corporation. To date, the Benefit Corporation is recognized by law in 34 US states and, since January 2016, also in Italy under the name 'Benefit Company'. In April 2018 Colombia and British Columbia were added to this list (Figure 18).[5]

---

[4] Extractive companies take more value from the ecosystem and the society than the one they return back with their activities, while regenerative companies (such as B Corps) do the opposite: through their activities, they use financial, human and natural resources to restore the ecosystem and the society while creating value for shareholders.

[5] Bianchi and Fasan, 2017; Supersociedades, 2018; Geiss, 2019.

Figure 18 The actual states and independent countries where the Benefit Corporation legal form is officially recognized

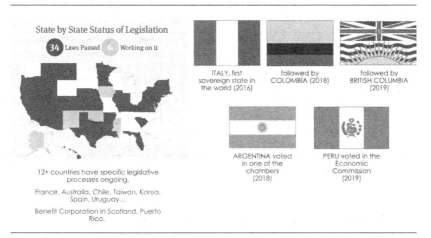

Source: B Lab, graphic elaboration by Nativa.

Table 5 presents the main differences between Certified B Corps and Benefit Corporations.

Table 5 Main differences between Certified B Corps and Benefit Corporations

Area	Certified B Corp	Benefit Corporation
Accountability	The administrators should take into account the effects of their decisions both on shareholders and stakeholders	The same as Certified B Corps
Transparency	The company has to publish a report encompassing its overall impact, using a third-party, independent standard	The same as Certified B Corps
Performance	Performance is certified by B Lab through the B Impact Assessment standard. It should be valued as >= 80 points out of 200	Self-assessed
Periodic verification	The certification should be reconfirmed every three years	The only periodic review is referred to transparency factors
Assistance	Access to a wide range of services, and support by B Lab	No formal support by B Lab
Use of Certified B Corp brands	Certified B Corps can use the Certified B Corp brands and logos for marketing purposes	Not available

Area	Certified B Corp	Benefit Corporation
Who can join	Every for-profit or high-social impact company, all over the world	Only in the US states and independent countries shown in Figure 18
Duties	The annual fee for B Corp certification varies according to the company's revenues, starting from €500	Within the USA, the administration fees range between $70 and $200. In Italy, fees are related to the modification of corporate governing documents so that they state the commitment to take into consideration the social and environmental impacts of the company's activities

Source: B Lab, Societabenefit.net, 2019.

8.3 The B Corp model and the fashion industry: case studies

As mentioned in the previous paragraphs, the adoption of the B Corp model allows companies to move from a profit-oriented paradigm to an approach aimed at creating a positive impact on society and the environment. This type of approach is a real opportunity for different types of business in various sectors, including the fashion industry. In this context, cases of interest stand out relating both to the adoption of innovative practices, and circular models of environment and resources management and cases of valorization, protection and support to community development. In Tables 6 to 9 we look at some of them in detail.

Table 6 Patagonia

Company and B Corp score	Patagonia – 151.5[6]
Identity[7]	Patagonia grew out of a small company that made tools for climbers. Alpinism remains at the heart of a worldwide business that still makes clothes for climbing—as well as for skiing, snowboarding, surfing, fly fishing, mountain biking and trail running.

---

[6] https://bcorporation.eu/directory/patagonia.
[7] https://www.patagonia.com/company-info.html (August 2019); https://www.patagonia.com/static/on/demandware.static/-/Library-Sites-PatagoniaShared/default/dw824fac0f/PDF-US/2017-BCORP-pages_022218.pdf (August 2019).

	The company's criteria for the best product rests on function, repairability, and, foremost, durability. Patagonia endeavors to build the best products, while causing no unnecessary harm to the planet or its inhabitants by: • designing and fabricating the highest quality products as defined by durability, multifunctionalism and non-obsolescence • designing and fabricating products that are easily repaired and made from materials that can be reused or recycled • designing and fabricating products with minimal impacts throughout the supply chain—including resource extraction, manufacturing and transportation—on water use, water quality, energy use, greenhouse gas emissions, chemical use, toxicity and waste • partnering with customers to take mutual responsibility for the life cycle of our products, including repair, reuse and recycling.
Why it became B Corp and Benefit Company[8]	"Patagonia is trying to build a company that could last 100 years," said founder Yvon Chouinard on the day Patagonia signed up. "Benefit corporation legislation creates the legal framework to enable mission-driven companies like Patagonia to stay mission-driven through succession, capital raises, and even changes in ownership, by institutionalizing the values, culture, processes, and high standards put in place by founding entrepreneurs."
BIA[9]	**Environment:** • On Black Friday, 2016, Patagonia pledged 100% of sales from Patagonia stores and patagonia.com to environmental organizations working to create positive change for the planet ($10 million). • 49% of fabrics by weight are made from recycled (29%) or renewable (20%) sources. **Collaborators:** • 500 employees are actively involved in grant making and advocacy, and decide which environmental organizations to support. • 2 on-site child development programs, one at Ventura, California, headquarters, the other at the customer service and distribution center in Reno, Nevada, for employees' children age 8 weeks through 9 years. • 95% of Patagonia moms returned to work after maternity leave (compared to the national average of 64%), thanks to on-site day care and other family-friendly practices. • 34% annual turnover in Patagonia retail compared to the national average of 72%, with 8% in the corporate headquarters compared to a national average of 10%. • 50% of Patagonia's workforce comprised of women, with women earning slightly more than the men, compared to 47% women at the average U.S. company.

---

[8] https://www.patagonia.com/b-lab.html (August 2019).
[9] https://www.patagonia.com/static/on/demandware.static/-/Library-Sites-PatagoniaShared/default/dw824fac0f/PDF-US/2017-BCORP-pages_022218.pdf (August 2019).

	Community: • 24% of all FY17 (F16/S17) products were Fair Trade Certified sewn. • 90% of Tier 1 finished-goods suppliers trained through the grievance system program to build effective and trustworthy two-way communication channels. • 425 speaking engagements—at which Patagonia employees shared information related to our culture, mission and operations—at universities, sustainability/eco- fashion events, outdoor industry gatherings, fabric/ textile conferences, HR conferences and others. **Governance:** • Patagonia is led by a female CEO, Rose Marcario. • 45% of Patagonia executives that are female, compared with the national average of 28%.
Key points[10]	Patagonia supports candidates who push hard for clean, renewable energy, restore clean water and air and turn away from risky, carbon-intensive fuels. For the last midterm election, Patagonia joined with the Creative Action Network and the Canary Project to run a crowd-sourced art campaign around the theme Vote the Environment. CAN and Canary run campaigns around causes, inviting artists to build collections of original, visual, meaningful art. Forty percent of the proceeds went directly to the artist, and thirty percent to HeadCount, a non-partisan organization that uses the power of music to register voters. Since 1985, Patagonia has also pledged 1% of sales to the preservation and restoration of the natural environment. 1% for the Planet is an alliance of businesses that understand the necessity of protecting the natural environment. They understand that profit and loss are directly linked to its health, and are concerned with the social and environmental impacts of industry. Furthermore, on Black Friday in 2016, Patagonia donated 100% of sales to grassroots organizations working to create positive change for the planet in their own backyards.
Website	Patagonia.com

---

[10] https://www.patagonia.com/vote-the-environment.html; https://www.patagonia.com/one-percent-for-the-planet.html; https://www.patagonia.com/100-percent-for-the-planet.html (August 2019).

Table 7 Davines

Company and B Corp score	Davines S.p.A. – 99.3
Identity	Founded in 1983 in Parma by the Bollati family, the Davines Group is a cosmetics company dedicated to the professional market. It specializes in the production of quality hair care products (under the Davines brand) for hairdressing salons, and skin care (under the Comfort Zone brand) for spas and beauty centres. While maintaining its Italian roots, today the group is an international entity present in 95 countries with branches in London, Paris, Mexico City, New York, Deventer and Hong Kong. The company produces, in its scientific laboratories, formulations elaborated with artisan spirit and scientifically developed through the most advanced cosmetic technologies, favouring ingredients of natural origin. The group's values are summarized in the concept of 'Sustainable Beauty', a balance between substance and form inspired by harmony, simplicity and good taste.
Why it became B Corp and Benefit Company	The Davines Group obtained the B Corp certification in 2016, highlighting its commitment to pursuing with coherence and transparency a path of ethical and environmental attention that has always been part of its DNA. Evolving its business model to have an even more positive impact on society and the planet, it wants to raise awareness among its stakeholders to do the same towards the creation of the best of the possible worlds.
BIA	**Environment:** • Increase in the share of recycled or recovered solid waste, including waste-to-energy process, equal to 91.9% of total solid waste; • Use of 100% of electricity from renewable resources in the Parma manufacturing facilities; • 71.4% renewable electricity used in the group's foreign branches; • 100% of turnover is generated from products that have CO2 equivalent (CO2e) offset packaging; • Carrying out of the SLCA (Strategic Life Cycle Assessment) analysis aimed at establishing the environmental and social impact over the entire product lifecycle, on products corresponding to 75.3% of turnover; • carrying out of the LCA (life cycle assessment) analysis aimed to quantify, according to specific scientific standards, the impact of the product at each stage of the product life cycle, on products corresponding to 16.2% of turnover; All the 7 offices of the Davines Group are carbon neutral. **Employees:** • 44% of managerial roles are held by women, guaranteeing equal opportunities among the highest corporate responsibility roles; • Strong drive of the company towards internationalization and sensitization of employees to the values of inclusion and difference, 201 employees are of non-Italian nationality; • 98% of the employees received a performance bonus as proof of their equal contribution to the success of the company; • 1380 hours are allocated to company volunteer projects carried out by employees in the social, environmental and cultural fields;

- 63.2% of Parma office managers and top-level managers at the branch offices have objectives that are linked to sustainability;
- Up to 4 "agile working" days per month of for all colleagues who wish to take them and whose job types allow them to do so.

Community:

Davines is committed to a continuous improvement of its supply chain, thanks to a process of measurement, awareness and careful selection of partners with whom the company works:

- 80.4% of suppliers measure their impact on the planet to increase their positive environmental and social impact;
- 43% have a company code of ethics;
- 49% offer additional benefits to their colleagues (in addition to legal requirements);
- 61% implement good energy management/reduction practices;
- Projects of territorial involvement dedicated to the city of Parma, where the company has its headquarters, have been launched through the creation of partnerships and synergies between the public and private sectors;
- Since 2014 at an international level, the "I Sustain Beauty" campaign dedicated to professional clients is active, bringing together 240 projects in the social, environmental and artistic fields from 21 countries around the world with the goal of supporting and spreading beauty;
- Understanding the importance of interdependence has inspired the company to share B Corp culture with its partners, with the hope that an ever-increasing number of partners join Davines on the path toward a sustainable future. In 2018, Davines count 6 certified B Corp partners and another 4 who are currently in the certification review phase.

Governance:

- Annual drafting of a "Sustainability Report" that includes all sustainable activities, presents the results achieved and the objectives that the company sets for the following year with a view to sharing and transparency towards its stakeholders;
- Dissemination of a business development model aimed at "prosperous longevity" based on balance and economic and financial sustainability and the uniqueness and attractiveness of brands.

Key points	The interdependence between the health and wellbeing of man and the planet is an important driver of ethics and sustainable development. Feeling responsible for change, the Davines Group is committed to a number of areas. Ensuring virtuous processes that include the reduction and recycling of its waste, a progressive choice with less impact and a more responsible design of its products, and the involvement of suppliers in improving environmental and social sustainability performance. Activating measures to combat the consequences of climate change, through the compensation of CO_2 from the production of packaging through reforestation projects in various parts of the world and the purchase of certified carbon credits. By favouring natural raw materials with low toxicity and highly biodegradable ingredients in the formulation of its products.

8 THE PURPOSE OF BUSINESS, B-CORPS AND BENEFIT CORPORATIONS

	Activating territorial involvement projects at international level through the 'I Sustain Beauty' campaign, collecting and rewarding social, environmental and artistic projects carried out by sector professionals all over the world, at local level involving Parma and its territory in particular, and in Italy in general through collaboration with its professional and non-professional clients in environmental marketing campaigns.
Websites	• Davines.com • comfortzone.it • isustainbeauty.com • sustaining-beauty.com

Table 8 MUD Jeans

Company and B Corp score	MUD Jeans International – 87.7
Identity	MUD Jeans was founded by Bert van Son, a fashion professional who in 2013 had a simple but brilliant idea: if we can rent cars, DVDs and books, why shouldn't we do it with clothes? Sustainability coincides with the company's business model, whose goal is to provide quality, ethical jeans to as many people as possible. Garments are rented for a monthly fee, and when they are worn out or you're just bored of wearing them, after 12 months you can return them and get more in return. MUD Jeans takes care of recycling old garments to create new ones. The transition from the concept of ownership to that of use is the foundation of the circularity of the system.
Why it became B Corp and Benefit Company	It is clear that the business concepts of MUD Jeans and the B Corp movement coincide: to create value for people and for the planet not in parallel, but through business activities. In 2015 the company was officially certified as B Corp, and in three of the following four years it won the Best for the World – Environment award, as proof of its commitment to reducing the environmental impact of the fashion sector.
BIA	It is not surprising that the MUD Jeans B Impact Assessment is highly rewarded in the environmental area, although this does not mean that the remaining impacts are neglected: **Environment**: • The circularity of the business model implies the conservation of the raw material, cotton, with all the benefits that follow in terms of saving water resources, climate-changing emissions, fertilizers and pesticides; • In the last three years, 300 million litres of water, 700,000kg of CO_2 and 12,000 pairs of jeans have been saved, otherwise destined for incineration or landfill. **Employees**: • Although the industry in which the company operates implies that most of the social impacts occur along the supply chain, MUD Jeans employees enjoy various benefits and a particular appreciation of the person beyond the professional role.

	Community: • All MUD Jeans are produced in the Tunisian Yousstex factory, which ensures high standards of sustainability and respect for workers; • The positive impact on the supply chain and the workers who are part of it is guaranteed through various measures: – A short chain with long-term relationships; – A code of conduct; – Collaboration with the Fair Wear Foundation to ensure that satisfactory salaries are paid along the supply chain; – 90% of Yousstex employees are women. **Governance:** • Officialization of the commitment to consider all stakeholders in the decision-making process; • High standards of transparency on practices, impacts and results of company activities.
Key points	MUD Jeans is a company that until a few years before its foundation seemed impossible: to operate successfully and sustainably in the fast fashion sector (the second most polluting in the world after that of fossil fuels), structuring the business model so that the growth in profitability of the company corresponds to a decrease in the environmental impact of the same. Circularity is becoming increasingly popular, particularly in the fashion sector where it is the main tool used to improve sustainability performance. MUD Jeans demonstrates how design theories and the ability to think outside the box allow it to operate successfully even in complex sectors, where historically big players have difficulty meeting the emerging values and ideals of the public.
Website	mudjeans.eu

8 The Purpose of Business, B-Corps and Benefit Corporations

Table 9 Elvis & Kresse

Company and B Corp score	Elvis & Kresse – 90.3
Identity	In 2005 the company started to design and manufacture luxury accessories using decommissioned fire hoses, allocating 50% of the profits to The Fire Fighters Charity. Today, the business has expanded to rescue 15 different waste materials, and has saved more than 200 tons of material from being sent to landfill. Elvis & Kresse also works with the Burberry Foundation to rescue offcuts from the production of Burberry leather goods. In this case, 50% of the profits are donated to Barefoot College. To date, Elvis & Kresse has created three scholarships to train female solar engineers at the Barefoot College. The company follows the Japanese principle of Kitsugi, the art of repairing ceramic objects through the use of gold in cracks. In the same way, objects such as fire hoses, which save lives all over the world every day, are given new dignity, thus producing objects with a much higher value.
Why it became B Corp and Benefit Company	Elvis & Kresse operated as a B Corp before the B Corp movement was born. It is a certified Social Enterprise too. The company's DNA consists of three core elements: rescuing materials, transforming them into awesome products and donating half of the proceeds to charity. Recognizing how the current economic system places the shareholder above the planet and its people, Elvis & Kresse identified the B Corp movement as the best way to challenge the status quo. Elvis & Kresse particularly love that all B Corps have to sign the Declaration of Interdependence and change their constitution to state that their shareholders are NOT more important than the planet or its people. The company also points out that 'being a B Corp is above all a source of joy: it is an optimistic and determined movement that is happy to roll up its sleeves, and to do so with a smile'.
BIA	**Environment:** • Obviously, basing one's production on waste materials has a positive impact in terms of circularity, waste reduction and energy use, which also has a positive impact on greenhouse gas emissions. **Collaborators:** • Elvis & Kresse also presents good practices from the point of view of the financial security of its employees, ensuring an adequate level of remuneration. **Community:** • 50% of the company's profits are earmarked for charitable organizations. In particular, 50% of the profits from the fire hose range is donated to The Fire Fighters Charity, in line with the philosophy from which the company was born. **Governance:** • The company has adopted various measures to maintain its social and environmental mission over time.

Key points	Elvis & Kresse is an excellent example of how sustainability can be embedded at the core of a business rather than on the CSR fringe. Their donations do not represent a solely philanthropic activity, but a real ideal link that allows the circular flow of capital. The loop is closed from both a social and an environmental point of view: value is obtained from materials that have saved lives, and it is returned to them after they have been reconditioned to increase their value. The concept of material recovery was then extended to other raw materials, demonstrating that this is a scalable and replicable business model that derives value from what is conventionally considered waste. This value is then redistributed in line with the company's objective of reducing waste while achieving multiple positive objectives. The Elvis & Kresse motto is: 'Do More, Be Better'.
Website	elvisandkresse.com

References

Bianchi, S. & Fasan, M. (2017). *L'azienda sostenibile. Trend, strumenti e case study.* Venice, Edizioni Ca' Foscari.

Geiss, B. (2019). 'British Columbia gets benefit company legislation.' Available at: https://www.coveadvisors.com

Societabenefit (2019). Available at: http://www.societabenefit.net

Supersociedades (2018). 'Nueva ley le da vía libre a la creación de empresas con vocación de beneficio social.' Available at: https://www.supersociedades.gov.co

9 The Future of Fashion

by *Francesca Romana Rinaldi*

> *Without technology humanity has no future,*
> *but we have to be careful that we don't*
> *become so mechanised that we lose our human feelings.*
> Dalai Lama Tenzin Gyatso

This chapter presents the views of several opinion leaders who discuss the future of fashion as we head towards 2030. The most innovative business models in the fashion sector will be based on a value proposition that integrates ethics, aesthetics and innovation, working on an omnichannel and transmedia storytelling approach, offering product customization, planning the activities for consumer participation in the company's value chain, digitalization, and use of technology in order to optimize the processes along the value chain, including production planning and forecast or manufacturing, trying for instance to minimize or, even better, to avoid unsold stock. Emerging technologies such as wearables, blockchain, IoT, AR, VR, 3D printing, nanomaterials, robotics, AI and machine learning are driving the industry towards the 4th Industrial Revolution.

We have arrived at the end of our journey across the different drivers of change; but some questions are still to be considered:

1. Which *technologies* will further disrupt the industry and drive business models towards higher sustainability in fashion? Is blockchain a buzzword or it will really be the internet of the future?
2. How is *automation* going to transform economies and the workforce?

Governments (see Box 24) and companies are trying to leverage the opportunities of Fashion 4.0 and face the related challenges.

Box 24 Towards the 4th Industrial Revolution: the case of Italy

The Plan 'Enteprise 4.0' of the Italian Ministry of Economic Development set policy objectives and instruments to achieve the '4th Industrial Revolution' whereby digitalization and breakthrough technologies change the way products, services and processes are put in place.

The policies were based on four pillars: 1) Support to digital investments; 2) Improving skills of workers; 3) Digital infrastructures, including 5G; 4) Digital services through mechanisms of competence centres and digital hubs.

The Directorate for International Industrial Cooperation, CSR, innovative start-ups and SMEs was focused on supporting digital investments. It has identified structural tools such as: patent box, fiscal credits for R&D expenditures and cyclical measures such as depreciation (until 2018) and hyper-depreciation for acquisitions of machinery and software. These tools were strictly related to investments of companies, including SMEs for intellectual properties, R&D and digitalization of production. At the same time with a holistic approach the Directorate promoted the birth and growth of innovative start-ups and SMEs.

The plan was neutral in terms of industries and technologies: digitalization can contribute also to improvements in the fashion industry.

In 2019 the Ministry of Economic Development launched new technology-targeted strategies to be defined thanks to the contribution of a task-force composed of experts and civil society representatives.

The targeted technologies were AI and blockchain and a new fund was created with the budget law to finance projects in this area.

Looking at the main benchmarks from the OECD analyses, Italy is quite strong compared to other countries in terms of automation.

The Directorate also focused on significant aspects of the fashion industry, such as traceability and transparency in supply chains, circular economy in relation with consumers and other stakeholders, incorporation of innovation in processes and products, for example on the new upcoming trend towards innovative products such as new textiles and new materials, new products incorporating themselves some innovations such as sentors and nanotechnologies.

Much can be done in terms innovation in the fashion industry to contribute to the implementation of the UN SDGs. In Italy there are many circular economy initiatives, especially regarding the use of waste from the industrial process to make new textiles. As for supply chain management, the Directorate started working on making the companies more aware of improving supply chain management, especially where Italian companies are part of long and international supply chains.

Since the Rana Plaza accident, the Directorate has participated in international initiatives such as the Sustainability Compact for Bangladesh, with the ILO and OECD, to make guidance to improve supply chain management.

The focus of this activity is to manage the risks of negative impacts through due diligence approaches and practices.

In this way the Directorate supports the UN/UNECE project on traceability in the garment sector financed by the EU. Traceability is a good tool to manage the supply chain; it is also to be understood that since the supply chain is quite complex, it is difficult for companies to trace their production and thus we welcome collective intiative lead by the private sector that can reduce costs and enhance results.

Sources: Interview with Maria Benedetta Francesconi, Dirigente Divisione VI – International Industrial Cooperation, CSR, Innovative Start-ups and SMEs, Italian Ministry of Economic Development: https://www.mise.gov.it/index.php/it/industria40

To forecast the future of fashion with any degree of precision is impossible: facing this challenge, this chapter will provide an idea about what the fashion industry in 2030 might look like.

9.1 How 4.0 technologies[1] can disrupt and support sustainable fashion?

In its 'Circular x Fashion Tech – Trend Report 2018' for the Global Change Award by H&M Foundation, Accenture explains in detail the main technologies that are supporting fashion companies in reducing the sustainability impact.

By Accenture's definition, the digital fashion technologies are based on communication, electronics and computer sciences. The physical ones are technologies that use physics, are related to the fundamental property of materials, nature's forces and energy, while the biological ones are focused on the function and structure of living organisms and their systems, as well as derivatives thereof.

---

[1] In this book 4.0 technologies include all technologies that are impacting on the Renewed Fashion Value Chain, not just in the manufactoring activity.

Accenture identifies the following nine main technologies:

Digital technologies
1. *Wearables*, defined as connected garments;[2]
2. *Circular Consumption Models*, including collaborative consumption platforms;
3. *Connected Supply Chain*, including blockchain and IoT.

Physical technologies
1. *3D Solutions*, such as printing and scanning;
2. *Nanomaterials*, smart fabrics that have novel capabilities, such as stain repulsion, increased durability, self-cleaning or ability to absorb pollutants;
3. *Robotics, including AI*, such as physical robots that can sort and collect waste, improve productivity and algorithms that can increase precision in forecasts and production planning.

Biological technologies
1. *Bio-based Materials*, biodegradable materials from biomass feedstocks and other organic components, such as bioplastics and cellulose fibres;
2. *Renewable Energy and Bioenergy*, derived from biomass or bioenergy feedstock;
3. *Biomimicry*, which means solving human challenges towards a higher sustainability by studying and imitating nature's best designs and processes, for instance, spider silk to produce biodegradable garments, artificial leather made from wood and altering cotton crops to enable faster growth and lessen need for water.

Even without a focus on the fashion industry and sustainability, Gartner, the leading IT research and advisory company, forecasts that blockchain, quantum computing, augmented analytics and AI will drive disruption and new business models. In addition to existing technologies, Gartner mentions the importance of immersive experiences (i.e. AR and VR) that

---

[2] Wearable technology devices that have a positive impact on quality of life, social setting and environment can include, for example, a fitness tracker that monitors health conditions.

could be especially relevant for 4.0 training and instore storytelling about who and what is behind the product.

An updated overview of the technologies that could be relevant in making the Fashion Industry 2030 more sustainable is presented in Table 10. One way of considering them is looking at how they impact on the processes, across the different activities of the Renewed Fashion Value Chain.

Table 10   Impact of 4.0 technologies for responsible innovation on the activities of the Renewed Fashion Value Chain

Activity/ Emerging technologies	FASHION 4.0 TECHNOLOGIES										
	Digital/physical technologies								Biological Technologies		
	Wearables	Blockchain	IoT	AR and VR	3D printing and knitting	Nanomaterials	Robotics	AI and machine learning	Bio-based materials	Renewable energy and bioenergy	Biomimicry
Sourcing of ingredients		X	X	X		X		X	X		X
Design and manufacture	X	X	X	X	X	X	X	X	X	X	X
Distribution and sales		X	X		X		X	X		X	
Communication and engagement	X	X	X	X	X		X	X			
Use, care and disposal	X	X	X	X		X		X			
Recycle and upcycle		X	X			X		X	X		X

Source: Author's elaboration.

4.0 technologies can improve the sustainability impact across the Renewed Fashion Value Chain. For example in the **Sourcing** activity, the presence of blockchain will increase transparency; IoT sensors will be common in agriculture to track and trace the agronomic practices and montitor eventual issues that take place upstream; VR will be used for virtual prototyping in order to reduce environmental impact; the use of AI will make the forecast more precise and will optimize sourcing; the use of nanomaterials will reduce the need for water and cleaning products, extending the product's durability; the use of bio-based materials will increase recycling rates, reduce waste, decrease the number of new input materials; and the use of biomimicry will avoid the use of chemical pigments for dyeing, reducing the use of non-biodegradable inputs.

Design and Manufacture activities will be the most affected by 4.0 technologies: the presence of wearables will increase capability of product tracking, decrease energy needs and reduce waste; blockchain will also increase the product traceability, making manufacturing more efficient; IoT technologies will guarantee higher traceability and better customization and optimization of the production; VR will be used for virtual prototyping in order to reduce environmental impact; AR will support in terms of 4.0 training, guaranteeing a reduced number of machinery-related accidents; 3D printing and knitting will guarantee a greater customization and higher utilization rate and will make feasible the just-in-time for lower risk of overstock; nanomaterials will require reduced need of water and cleaning products; robotics, AI and machine learning will minimize waste and optimize production; the use of bio-based materials and renewable energy and bioenergy will minimize waste; biomimicry will avoid the use of chemical pigments for dyeing, reducing the use of non-biodegradable inputs.

Distribution and Sales activities will be affected especially by: blockchain, thanks to a higher traceability and more efficient logistics; IoT, thanks to the presence of a connected wardrobe for higher efficiency; AR & VR, enhancing the instore storytelling on the invisible behind the visible; robotics, that will guarantee a reduced need of CO_2 emissions from transportation; AI & machine learning, that will guarantee to work on personalized recommendations; use of renewable energy and bioenergy, that will reduce the environmental impact also for this activity.

Communication and Engagement activities will be affected especially by wearables, blockchain, IoT, AR and VR, 3D printing, robotics, AI and machine learning thanks to a better understanding of customer needs. Through the 'one customer view' approach, the fashion industry 2030 will be able to engage much more (and much better) the customers. Blockchain will be especially helpful in this activity in making one-to-one communications and provide rewards and incentives to consumers.

Use, Care and Disposal activities will be affected especially by wearables that will guarantee and increased health of users; blockchain will guarantee one-to-one communication and provide rewards and incentives to the consumers; IoT will track product usage and connected wardrobes will guarantee higher efficiency and increased utilization rate of clothes; AR and VR will enable immersive storytelling; nanomaterials will extend the product durability; AI and machine learning will enable much more recommendations during the use, care and disposal phase.

Recycle and Upcycle activities will be affected by blockchain and IoT, thanks to an increased traceability. AI and machine learning, nanomaterials, bio-based materials and biomimicry will minimize waste, and guarantee increased recycling rates.

Table 11 lists examples of technologies for responsible innovation and their sustainability impact.

Box 25 focuses especially on a selection of the digital and physical technologies – blockchain, IoT, AR and VR, AI and machine learning – to highlight their relevant impact to many of the Renewed Fashion Value Chain activities.

Table 11 Examples of 4.0 technologies for responsible innovation and sustainability impact on the Renewed Fashion Value Chain

| | FASHION 4.0 TECHNOLOGIES ||||||||| Biological technologies |||
| | Digital/physical technologies |||||||| | Biological technologies |||
	Wearables	Blockchain	IoT	AR and VR	3D printing and knitting	Nanomaterials	Robotics	AI and machine learning	Bio-based materials	Renewable energy and bioenergy	Biomimicry
Examples	Connequ Tracker by Piquadro; Fitbit	1TrueID; Provenance	Amazon Echo and Echo Look	Impersive, Centric 8 (Centric Software)	Adidas-FutureCraft 4D Shoe, Reebok- Liquid Factory, Uniqlo 3D U-Knit	Dropel, Hydrop	aha, powered by Flytrex; Li&Fung sewbots; Uniqlo 'Pepper' robot	heuritech, Stitch Fix	Vegea, Frumat	n/a	Biosteel, R.A.W.
Sustainability impact	• Product tracking • Decreasing energy needs and reduced waste • Increased health of users	• Higher transparency • Higher traceability (more efficient manufacturing and logistics through real time logistics, waste management and recycling)	• Connected wardrobe for higher efficiency and increased utilization rate • Higher traceability and higher control in sourcing and supply chain (industrial IoT)	• Reduced environmental impact and waste thanks to digital prototyping • Reduced accidents with machineries thanks to 4.0 training instore storytelling	• Higher customisation and higher utilization rate • Minimisation of waste • Just in time and lower risk of overstock	• Reduced need of water and cleaning products • Extended product durability	• More efficient forecasts, reduced stock, minimized waste • Reduced need of CO_2 emissions from transport	• Personalized recommendations • More efficient forecasts, reduced stock, minimized waste	• Increased recycling rates, reduced waste, decrease in the number of new input materials	• Reduced waste by deriving biodegradable energy from biological materials • Reduced CO_2 emissions	• Avoided use of chemical pigments for dyeing, reduced use of non-biodegradable inputs

Source: Author's elaboration.

Box 25 Notes on blockchain, IoT, VR, AI and machine learning technologies

Blockchain[3]

"Blockchain could be the new internet. When internet started there was exactly the same discussion around it. For example the general approach towards online sales was sceptical due to the consideration that the solution could not be applicable on large scale. Amazon experienced challenges and difficult periods before turning into an established solution. Blockchain is at a similar stage today as internet was in late 80s, early 90s. The technology is rather complex and it is at an early stage today but blockchain is so unique because allows to store decentralized information in a secured way without the possibility to change the stored data afterwards. This option is relevant to provide a tangible proof supporting the company claims. The second, even more important, feature is the chance to combine the stored information with a value - the value to the owner of information, the value of the transaction, the value of impact – a significant value such as the well-known bitcoins that can be used for trading. Blockchain used just as a database wouldn't be a development. What makes blockchain technology really powerful is the combination of having a secured information exchange and adding value thanks to the tokens (a concept pioneered by bitcoins). It's a combination of possibilities that makes it unique but also so complex. The key goal of blockchain community is the empowerment of decentralized units. Currently most information is administered by proprietary platforms – actually the owners of the information – accessible only with a membership. Through blockchain we would completely change this approach empowering our partners in the supply chain so that they can disclose the information not only to a third party – a proprietary platform – but directly to the brands retailers and any other stakeholder – ensuring complete transparency and reliability of the information they publish. The aim is to offer in the future a multistakeholder shared platform that different actors (partners, NGO, development agencies) can join to guarantee intensified collaboration, traceability and transparency over the value chain. The consumers could be involved as well. Once you have transparency and you start disclosing to your consumer secured and validated information showing the value of sustainable practices, you can launch a loyalty program using the tokens as a loyalty tool: when customer buys a garment the brand can provide him/her value through a token that he can use to buy new clothes or to support an improvement project in the brand's supply chain. The tokens function as an ideal instrument for loyalty programs, which can foster long-term partnerships between business partners and build trust between brands and their final consumers.[4] Embracing the holistic approach you can ex-

---

[3] Extract from an interview of the author with Heinz Zeller, Principal Sustainability of a leading premium fashion brand.

[4] Source: https://www.globalfashionagenda.com/blockchain-unlocking-the-value-chain-for-better-traceability

perience the power of an ecosystem based on blockchain where you can engage with your consumers and the consumers will be able to "value" the processes and the product sustainability, learning about social and environmental benefits or improvement programs in the supply chain. The consumers then can actively engage again back in company's supply chain reinvesting the token and contributing to a better future. On the other side of the spectrum, tokens, already used today for crowdfunding, will become an ideal way to connect improvement projects within such an ecosystem to all partners (donors and receivers) in the value chain in a fully transparent way either publicly sponsored or as a public-private partnership.[5] This is an extraordinary innovation holding the potential to change the industry and to design a better future."

IoT – Connected wardrobes[6]

In 2019, connected wardrobes do not exist, but in 2030 it is likely that we will have an app that could show consumers the total usage of each product in their wardrobe, which could be filtered according to different attributes such as 'occasion of use', 'quality', 'sustainability score' and other features. This app could then recommend the consumers what to shop for according to product usage, sharing info on which colours, fabrics, patterns or fit that she/he uses/wears the most. The app could even provide total look recommendations or suggest how to combine different garments and inform about unused products that could be recycled.

VR

VR has become an immersive tool through which companies can communicate and inform. The application of virtual and cross reality in fashion is great, particularly when visual and engaging experiences increase efficiency, productivity, safety and sustainability.

Impersive (https://impersive.com/) is a VR content production company. By using VR they create an interactive and extremely realistic environment that provides a fully enclosed experience, incorporating auditory and visual feedback. This enables potential customers to experience the creation of some of the most iconic items, to explore the factory or even the whole supply chain, to view a library of fashion shows by sitting front row and they can be anywhere in the world while they are doing so. By wearing a VR headset the person 'acquires a body' and actively participates in the story becoming an integral part of the experience. By using VR as a medium, immersive virtual reality storytelling is probably the most deeply interactive form of communication. This enables fashion brands to: demonstrate product attributes, features, functionality; communicate the brand's sustainable mission at

---

[5] Source: https://www.globalfashionagenda.com/blockchain-unlocking-the-value-chain-for-better-traceability-2/#

[6] Adapted from https://fashionretail.blog/2019/04/15/what-if-sustainability-starts-in-your-closet/.

point of sale; immerse users in an entertainment experience and add excitement at pop-up events for social media sharing; help consumers make more informed choices; revolutionize the way businesses approach training; add a new, more immersive and exhilarating dimension to traditional print and video storytelling.

AI and machine learning
AI and machine learning could improve production, trends and sales forecast, thus reducing the overstock.

Heuritech is a start-up especially focused on improving trends forecast.[7]
In the era of social media, influence hasshifted to real-world influencers through millions of images on Instagram and other visual platforms. This presents a tremendous opportunity for brands to better understand the state of the market and tap into future trends. Heuritech's visual processing detects and predicts what's coming next. Products, brands, colors, patterns, shapes.
From spotting the next big trend to creating more accurate demand and sales forecasts, Heuritech informs and improves every step of the fashion lifecycle through analyzing pictures on social media from influencers and consumers. More in detail the sustainability impact is related to optimizing the product assortment with best-selling trends and products, ensuring the relevance of timing and product offer for future launches, improving the accuracy of sales forecasts and demand planning to produce more sustainably.
The belief is that Big Data can help fashion to be more sustainable for long term profitability.

9.2 An automated fashion industry?

In the 2017 report 'A Future that Works: Automation, Employment and Productivity' McKinsey Global Institute, business and economics research arm of McKinsey & Company, confirmed that in the new frontier, automation technologies including robotics and AI have advanced rapidly: according to the report 'half of today's work activities could be automated by 2055, but this could happen up to 20 years earlier or later depending on the various factors, in addition to other wider economic conditions'.[8]

While efficiency for businesses will increase, some key social issues on employment will become crutial for policy makers, such as rethinking education and training, income support and safety nets and transition support.

---

[7] The following paragraph is extracted from https://www.heuritech.com.
[8] McKinsey Global Institute, 2017.

"The common consideration is that digital development and automation can have a negative impact on overall CSR development in terms of reduced workplaces but actually we are going to switch from a low tech-labour intensive approach versus a high tech-knowledge intensive approach. In the fashion & textile community there is an ongoing discussion since digital development is introducing an innovative way to produce goods, a highly automated production based on computerization, robots, specialized machineries. Of course, replacing workers with robots could be a risk for employment in the countries were the fashion brands produce goods, especially in low developed countries such as Bangladesh. The use of robots in their production facilities must have the main objective of enhancing flexibility and efficiency with no or limited reduction of the working force. The amount of production steps executed by a single operator should be reduced, so that the worker can focus on key tasks and be more productive. An extreme approach is offered by Adidas SPEEDFACTORY where advanced digital technologies are applied to create the future performance footwear in an efficient way. Some main advantages of the introduction of specialized machineries are a high and continuous precision, faster and flexible production, reduced lead-time but there is also a third dimension, the environmental impact. Digital development can have a positive impact on the environment thanks to a better plan (less or no risk dispositions) and therefore a lower use of resources. The production left-overs will be reduced and the energy efficiency increased because, even though automation means more machines in the production lines, the new equipment are often more efficient and require lower resource consumption. After having performed an evaluation of the investments for sustainable innovation, it's not easy to define which is the best solution to implement whether a high tech-knowledge intensive approach or a low tech-labour intensive approach – it depends very much on the regional socio-economic conditions.

Development solutions based on **high technology and high knowledge** level are efficiency driven and ensure faster and higher integration and their ideal conditions are in medium to high-wage countries since relevant capital investments are required. The knowledge transfer to be performed is enormous so it's fundamental to work based on long-term partnerships. The potential downside could be a higher energy consumption due to the increased use of equipment and automation.

The opposite approach, **labor intensive with low usage of technologies**, is typically applied in low wage countries creating a social benefit of increased employment. The investments required are minimum, the knowledge level basic. That's a solution generally adopted at the initial stage of industrial development or at the beginning of a new partnership in developing countries. The downside could be a higher risk of social and environmental issues.

As a third dimension, we can identify the **natural resource intensity** where the natural resources can be a cost factor. The consumption of natural resources can help to create socio-economic benefits such as farming but impacts negatively on the natural resources (air, water, land) that will lead, if not well managed, to increased social costs. Therefore, **efficiency** is a main driver also for the natural resource conservation and training programs need to be provided to improve knowledge for reducing the environmental impact. The choice should be based on criteria related to the macroeconomics, the availability of specific resources (natural, human and financial capital) in the country, the level of development, etc…There is always an ideal solution for a specific environment, a specific country, factory, company. Technological development is capital intensive since the innovative technologies are very expensive but technology becomes quickly cheaper and accessible so there is a conflict with the cost of labor and the availability of technology. Training to move people to the next competence level is required. We can conclude that digital development is positive but also risky for some of the developing countries." [9]

Companies and policy makers need concrete actions to educate the new generations to get ready for automation, as confirmed by the '2018 Deloitte Millennial Survey – Millennials disappointed in business, unprepared for Industry 4.0'. The report states that 'in a fragmenting social and political environment, with Industry 4.0 driving profound changes, many Millennials are exhibiting a marked desire for reassurance. They feel pessimistic about the prospects for political and social progress, along with concerns about safety, social equality and environmental sustainability. While young workers believe that business should consider stakeholders' interests as well as profits, their experience is of employers prioritizing the

---

[9] Extract from an interview of the author with Heinz Zeller, Principal Sustainability of a leading premium fashion brand.

bottom line above workers, society and the environment, leaving them with little sense of loyalty.'[10]

Getting ready for automation will be a crucial aspect to get back the loyalty of new generations of employees (and consumers) by 2030.

9.3 Towards fashion industry 2030

9.3.1 *Drivers of change, advantages for the companies and consumer benefits*

Social issues are arising. The environment is suffering. Consumers are buying more and using less. Inventory levels are increasing. A concrete revolution is needed to see a different fashion industry by 2030.

Going 'behind sustainability' is a must. Sustainability, as a term, must be used if, and only if, companies are able to measure results on how transparency and traceability, circularity and collaborative consumption have reshaped the processes along the activities of their value chains.

Transparency and traceability. Circularity. Collaborative consumption.

As discussed, some clear signs are showing that those drivers will be the catalysts of the urgent change needed, creating 'shared value'[11] for many stakeholders, including the planet and people. They will have a strong impact on the different activities of the Renewed Fashion Value Chain, generating both concrete advantages for the fashion players and relevant consumer benefits (Figure 19), such as:

1. *Sourcing of Ingredients*: companies will be able to manage the issue of the scarcity of resources; consumers will have full visibility of raw materials;
2. *Design and Manufacture*: companies will optimize production, reducing unsold stocks; consumers will have a more tailored offer;
3. *Distribution and Sales*: companies will optimize logistics; consumers will have many more options than in the past (buy new or second-hand, swap, rent, lease);

---

[10] Deloitte, 2018.
[11] Porter and Kramer, 2011.

Figure 19 Company benefits and consumer advantages across the activities of the Renewed Fashion Value Chain

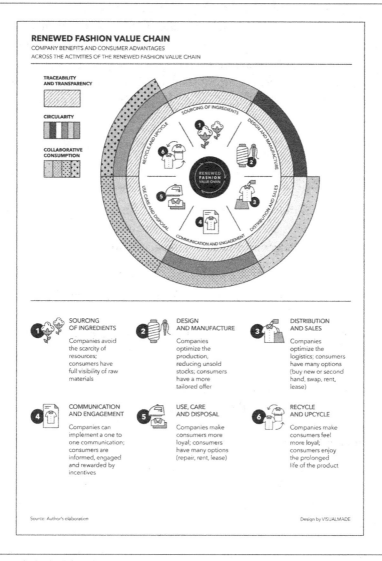

Source: Author's elaboration.

4. *Communication and Engagement*: companies will be able to implement a one-to-one communication; consumers will be more informed, engaged and rewarded by incentives;
5. *Use, Care and Disposal*: companies will avoid the scarcity of resources and make consumers more loyal; consumers will have many options to extend the life of the products (repair, rent, lease);
6. *Recycle and Upcycle*: companies will make consumers feel more loyal; consumers will enjoy the prolonged life of their products.

9.3.2 New rules of the game for the Fashion Industry by 2030

Thanks to more than three years' research collecting the points of view of managers and experts and collecting reports on the evolution of business models and consumers' needs in fashion, this final section shows relevant quotes from experts and opinion leaders that could interpret or even forecast the rules of the game of fashion industry 2030:

1. Having traceable and transparent value chains
2. Involving the consumer in a take-make-remake model to prolong product life
3. Reading and interpreting data so technologies can enhance human creativity
4. Granting consumer-centricity, engagement and inclusivity
5. Going from products to services
6. Making profits without harming the environment or society

1. *Having traceable and transparent value chains*

By 2030, fashion companies will try to achieve 100% transparency and traceability, facing the challenges related to tracing global supply chains – till Tier 4 – and sharing interactive contents related to what is behind the products through smart labels.

> *To make solid and reliable sustainability claims, designers, brands and business actors in the fashion industry need to know their clients and suppliers. For that to happen we must achieve 100% transparency and traceability of the value chain. This is key for us to know where and how our clothes are made, and take truly responsible choices.*
> Maria Teresa Pisani, Acting Head, Sustainable Trade and Outreach Unit, United Nations Economic Commissions for Europe

9 THE FUTURE OF FASHION   167

> *The future of the Italian fashion industry is in global markets. Thus the industry will be more sophisticated in terms of quality of products and services, more digitalized and automated to increase productivity and sales and more sustainable to reduce the costs of resources and respond to the request of the market/consumers.*
> *As for sustainability, to be accountable towards consumers a to communicate sustainability, credible and effective transparency on firm's processes and content of products (including environmental and social content) will be crucial.*

Maria Benedetta Francesconi, Dirigente Divisione VI – International Industrial Cooperation, CSR, Innovative Start-ups and SMEs, Italian Ministry of Economic Development

> *I think that digital will be an enabler for a lot of our actual problems: consumers will be able to engage better with brands, there will be better measuring of CSR performance, there will be better visibility for the supply chain thanks to technologies like blockchain ecosystems. It will be a pleasant change, getting nearer the right direction, enabling solutions that will support evolution towards a better and more sustainable Fashion Industry.*

Heinz Zeller, Principal Sustainability at a leading premium fashion brand

> *On the technical and operational side the path is rather clear: Sustainability will be one of the main driving factor of future successful companies; technologies like blockchain will revolution the way we purchase but also will allow consumer to deep dive into the Fashion Brands supply chains and the secrecy we experience today about how our products are made and where they come from won't be possible any longer. Mass customization will also become feasible both for large companies and small ones. This will allow better management of stock levels and investments. Direct to consumer will become the main distribution business model and also due to the implementation of the above blockchain, most 'middle men' will either have to change model or will likely disappear.*

Nicola Giuggioli, Founder and CEO Eco-Age

2. *Involving the consumer in a take-make-remake model to prolong product life*

Fashion companies will involve consumers in their circular value chains, giving them many options to prolong the life of the product. Companies will deal with a bigger consumer segment that will value more quality than quantity.

> *We, at Fashion for Good, are aiming to change the fashion industry from a 'take-make-waste industry' to a 'take-make-remake industry'. We try to do this with our cooperative partners by scaling and implementing sustainable technologies which*

could be related to materials or circular business models. We believe that those innovations will help changing fashion and turn it into an industry where both people and planet can flourish.
Anne-Ro Klevant Groen, Communications Manager Fashion for Good

In my opinion the main difference between the fashion industry in 2019 and in 2030 is the one between new and used. Today the difference is still strong but I think that by 2030 it will be completely obsolete. I also think the industry could be much more distributive, with a lot of start-ups and small companies providing very different services for clothing and much more creativity.
François Souchet, Project Manager at Ellen MacArthur Foundation

Innovation will play a more central role in the fashion industry of the future, especially looking at the technologies, the innovative tools that are already available to the markets. I think models such as circular economy or 'leasing' in general are becoming more prominent and will play even a more important role. I also think that transparency will become more important and customers will all be more accountable for their actions. I think that sustainability will become more the norm, rather than a besides element, as it is now.
Eva Engelen, CSR responsible at MUD Jeans

I think we will see many of the best-in-class technologies that are already in use being more widely adopted. We will understand that sustainability is in no way a compromise for aesthetics. We will be using more renewable resources instead of non-renewable ones, and using these materials in smarter, more efficient ways. We will see the development of products that are truly circular – ones that are completely regenerative, and throughout the entire production process. This wave of conscious consumerism is bound to only increase. We will still see people turning to fashion as something that is fun and inspiring but with a greater level of awareness about how and where something was made. We will finally comprehend that less is more, by valuing quality way more over quantity. And I hope we will see an end to the idiotic practice of overproduction, linked to a senseless fashion cycle.
Simon Giuliani, Global Marketing Director Candiani Denim

First of all, I hope and believe that by 2030 all stakeholders in the fashion industry will be more aware about the topic of sustainability in fashion as well as all other sectors that we are touched by in our everyday lives. The already-existing trends such as upcycling, redesign and revamping of unsold products will become more common while more and more companies will pledge to abolish the practice of incinerating unsold stock or fabric and will find alternate ways of redirecting them back into the supply chain. There are already some examples that should inspire the industry's big players, like some brands emerging initiatives in which vulnerable young workers

> are employed in stores that sell unsold stock. *The increased attention to social and environmental issues, both arising within the industry and coming as a demand from consumers, will lead to the development of projects that aim at reducing the supply chain's carbon footprint and at enhancing its fairness in terms of workers' rights and wellbeing. In this, the practice of outsourcing will decline, allowing for 'Made in Italy' to have a broad comeback.*
> Anna Fiscale, President of Progetto Quid

> *Creativity, Variety and Novelty have driven so far how we create and consume fashion. I have no doubts that sustainability will be the 4th force to drive the industry in the next years. New Materials, New Technologies, New Business Models will be the enablers and pillars of the incoming fashion industry revolution. There is an ever increasing number of consumers that do not tolerate ignorance of these values. This means we are not talking about an ethical mission anymore, but a fundamental of business survival and growth opportunity in the coming years.*
> Andrea Ruzzi, European Fashion Lead, Managing Director at Accenture Italy & Europe

3. Reading and interpreting data so that technologies can enhance human creativity

Fashion companies will leverage on a big number of consumer data: thanks to AI it will be possible to craft effective user experiences, where all stakeholders will be active in the fashion value chains.

> *Robotics will change the way we understand the world. Every product, every human relation will be modulated by the presence of robots. Fashion will not be excluded from these changes, and will have to find ways to continue to excel human creativity.*
> Emanuele Micheli, President Scuola di Robotica, CEO Madlab 2.0

> *The fashion industry in 2030 will be strongly impacted by AI. In particular, intelligent technologies will let companies achieving a better understanding of their customers, by identifying in real-time their will and the characteristics each product should have. Other AI technological capabilities, such as conversational interfaces, advanced demand forecasting, image-based search and smart apps will also make an impact on the fashion industry. At the same time, connections between AI and human capabilities (creativity and ingenuity among the most relevant ones) will be the main challenge for the fashion players in the next years.*
> Fabio Foglia, Co-founder at MarketMind Research and Academic Fellow Bocconi University

> *The way to implement a circular fashion value chain will pass through traceability of products and processes. The security and integrity of information will be guaranteed by the adoption of verifiable smart contracts. This complex decentralized network will produce a big mass of data and thanks to AI it will be possible to produce an effective user experience, where all stakeholders can be active in the fashion value chain.*
> Niccolò Desenzani, Data Scientist Manager and Blockchain Expert Faberbee

4. *Granting consumer-centricity, engagement and inclusivity*

Fashion companies will put consumers' needs at the centre through product customization, on-demand collections, the omnichannel approach, transmedia storytelling and one-to-one communication. The industry will be much more inclusive.

> *The Fashion Industry in 2030 will see quality as a commodity and sustainability as a must. The new generations, particularly women, the consumers of the future, will be more interested in collecting many information from the websites, will choose with a buy less, buy better criterion. Specifically Generation Z will pay a premium price for those brands that will be able to communicate and show that their product could be more sustainable than the others. For the new generations it is very important that all the products have a storytelling that will include sustainability as the main focus.*
> Erika Andreetta, Partner PwC, Retail & Consumer Goods Consulting Leader

> *Fashion Industry 2030: massive diversity. I really want to see a totally different scenario. I want to see mending clothes in every corner. I want to see young designers and their diverse collections, designing different systems. Take-back schemes, swishing and sharing. I want to see different opportunities such as renting and swapping. But above all, I want to see the kind of inclusivity, the kind of originality that we don't have now. Our future is going to be about being more individualistic, smaller perhaps: rather than scaling up we should be replicating, as nature does.*
> Orsola de Castro, Co-founder of Fashion Revolution

> *I think in ten years from now more businesses will lead by example and more consumers will increasingly put pressure on companies to implement responsible practices in their business and supply chain. Therefore I am carefully optimistic. I just hope that the transition will be fast enough.*
> Yannick Meijers, Sales Manager Eastern Europe & MEA at Patagonia

> *Science fiction has always predicted dystopian worlds with uniforms and no space for personal identities. I do not think that creativity will die in 2030 but I am convinced that the future of the fashion industry will be built necessarily through the culture of making products that respect people and the planet. There is no other alternative for us to survive. Our duty (as managers) is to promote education and awareness through technical schools and teach to the young generation the sustainable way of making products. We will buy less in 2030 but, I am sure, we will buy differently. Customers will not be passive in the relation with brands and their supply chain. They will become proactive by customizing the products they love directly using hi-tech traceable platforms. The challenge for all of us is to become inclusive and to evolve accordingly.*
> Giorgio Ravasio, Country Manager, Vivienne Westwood Italy

> *The fashion industry in 2030 will be empowered by technology and human interactions. Each garment will have its 'digital twin' which will allow and enhance the interactions between final customer, product and firms. Products will be highly personalized and tailored according to real-time customer preferences. Stores will not be any more 'Point of Sale' but points of experience and co-creation. Supply chains and firms will need to be more sustainable and transparent, allowing customers to visit their plants, ensuring product authenticity during the complete product lifecycle, including second-hand markets.*
> Iolanda D'Amato, lecturer in Operations and Supply Chain Management and consultant

5. *Going from products to services*

Fashion companies will go from producing and distributing products to offering more personalized services such as reparing, renting and recommerce. In the future our wardrobes will be connected.

> *The notion of a linear economy is now obsolete. The future, instead, is circular and locates its natural mission in the building of shared value. Technology offers concrete solutions, such as blockchain, which will contribute to a future in which every piece of clothing will have a 'talking', digital label. One that can tell the story of how a particular item has been produced. Not only: the transition towards a sustainable and circular model also means transforming 'products' into 'services', rethinking materials, their lifecycle, the possibility of deconstructing and then reusing them. Without forgetting social aspects, which won't simply need to be mitigated, but integrated in a circular vision that generates positive impacts for entire communities.*
> Enea Roveda, CEO LifeGate

> *Making predictions when changes happen faster and faster is hard. However, from my perspective as connoisseur of the technology applied to fashion, what I do believe is that technology increasingly will pervade the fashion industry as enabling tool to make processes more efficient and effective, but technology will still be not a visible part of the final fashion item. Considering the final customers, I expect the fashion consumption bulimia will evolve into a more conscious consumption directed towards high quality: more durable garments, service-based consumptions such as short- and long-term rental and in general more sustainable approach towards the fashion consumption at large.*

Giusy Cannone, CEO Fashion Technology Accelerator

> *I personally believe that in 2030 consumers will have more and more a mixed wardrobe made by owned, second hand and rented products. To meet this needs, brands will not only integrate circular consumption business models into their primary channels, but they will manage them with the same level of relevance as direct owned channels. For example: consumers will find the rental price close to the sale price in the price tag of an item, as it is happening in the automotive sector.*

Paola Sironi, Fashion consultant at ACIN

6. *Making profits without harming the environment or society*

Fashion companies will integrate aesthetics, ethics and responsible innovation.

> *Everything in our culture must change in the next ten years to respond to the sustainability challenge. The very meaning of business must change: by 2030 profits made at a social or environmental cost will be hard to justify and new regenerative paradigms such as the B Corp will become absolutely normal. Many fashion businesses will disappear in this turmoil. Others will become future fit and lead the great transition.*

Eric Ezechieli, Co-founder, Nativa, first B Corp and Benefit Corporation in Europe

> *Society today is inner-directed and looking for values to navigate through life. We are all seeking for a truthful blueprint for a responsible living which won't deprive ourselves and future generations of our elemental sources of happiness. And the fashion industry in 2030, in the way clothes will be produced and consumed, will be a reflection of this. It will be the result of today's increasing awareness of the threats we face as humans, if we don't realign our habits with the needs of our planet and*

people. And it will be in the hands of the players who, with their choices in terms of sustainable development, are today casting a vote for the preservation of life. Working to embrace in the design process dynamics of circular economy and to build valuable supply chains.

Matteo Ward, Co-founder and CEO of WRÅD

I think that the fashion of the future should be based on the concept of the Third Paradise: the First Paradise is Nature, the Second Paradise is made of Artificial Life and the Third Paradise will be based on the connection between Nature and Artificial Life, connected to have a new balance that will be the Human future. We have the necessity of considering that fashion that until now was mainly based on Aesthetic meanings, needs a new integration between aesthetics and ethics, Artefact and Nature together in order to create a new balance. That is the creation. And creation is something that fashion has to deal with.

Michelangelo Pistoletto, contemporary artist and founder of Cittadellarte – Fondazione Pistoletto

References

Accenture, H&M Foundation (2018). 'Circular x Fashion Tech – Trend Report 2018'. Available at: https://www.accenture.com/t20180327t110326z__w__/us-en/_acnmedia/pdf-74/accenture-gca-circular-fashiontech-trend-report-2018.pdf

Deloitte (2018). '2018 Deloitte Millennial Survey – Millennials disappointed in business, unprepared for Industry 4.0'. Available at: https://www2.deloitte.com/content/dam/Deloitte/global/Documents/About-Deloitte/gx-2018-millennial-survey-report.pdf

Global Fashion Agenda (2019). Available at: https://www.globalfashionagenda.com/blockchain-unlocking-the-value-chain-for-better-traceability-2/#

McKinsey Global Institute (2017). 'A Future that Works: Automation, Employment and Productivity'. Available at: https://www.mckinsey.com/~/media/mckinsey/featured%20insights/Digital%20Disruption/Harnessing%20automation%20for%20a%20future%20that%20works/MGI-A-future-that-works-Executive-summary.ashx

Porter, M.E. & Kramer, M. R. (2011). 'Creating shared value', *Harvard Business Review*, 89(1/2) (January/February 2011), 62–77.

Afterword

by *Matteo Ward*

How did fashion become unsustainable? How did we all become unconscious supporters of a system engineered to make a few people richer and the rest of us poorer – in a stressed environment now at risk? Surely we didn't ask for fashion to become such a damaging industry and did not wish this for ourselves. So what happened?

In the 70's George Akerlof published a paper titled "The Market for Lemons: Quality Uncertainty and the Market Mechanism", depicting how information asymmetry between buyers and sellers in any given market ultimately leads to the supremacy of lower quality goods (what Akerlof in his essay refers to as lemons) over higher quality ones. Is this why we - having ignored the true environmental and social cost of our clothes - have our wardrobes now stuffed with chemical heavy, unhealthy, unrecyclable and unethical clothing? I believe so.

I spent the first 9 years of my work-life selling clothes and my personal and professional success depended on my capability to inspire and drive my teams to sell more and more of them every single day. Would I have held myself accountable to different parameters had I been informed about the broader consequences of the fashion industry? Absolutely, and I am sure it is the same for the rest of us.

The problem now is that our market, as a consequence of such information asymmetry, is undeniably saturated with Akerlof's lemons, leaving us with nothing other than one possible output: a poor-quality lemonade. An unhealthy set of market-induced ingredients which for decades we have blended to satisfy our thirst for growth and short-term pleasure – de facto stripping all of the stakeholders involved (from customers to industry insiders) of the incentives to ask the kind of critical questions which would have unfolded the unequivocal dichotomy between what we hold most important – creating a better future for ourselves and others – and what we have been actually doing to achieve the same.

And isn't this one of the greatest paradoxes of our times? A real crisis, personal and systemic, which today touches every industry and sphere of life, but also a situation which we should (and must, as our life depends on it!) embrace as our best opportunity for progress with a creative and open mindset. Because whether in finance, sales, marketing or product design today we are all called to re-imagine the formulas within which we are operating. Using design as a driver for innovation and change.

I share in this the opinion of Ranny Ramakers, founder and theorist of the Dutch Droog Design movement, that relevant design, without compromising on beauty, must act as a catalyst for positive change and discourage consumerism. A connotation which, when properly incorporated into the value proposition of a company, elevates the brand to the status of über brand as defined by Wolfgang Schäfer.

A company focused on making its outputs the tangible manifestation of these principles of design is paving the way for its successful transition through the 4th Industrial Revolution. An era which is defined by one key question: "how can we justify making and selling more clothes people do not really need, using more resources we do not really have?". Answering this means bringing to the table more than simple sourcing strategies of more responsible materials or launching social give-back compensating schemes – we must embrace the challenge with an holistic and inclusive approach for all stakeholders involved. Because giving our work the real power to catalyze a revolution means re-defining business paradigms and the economics of an entire industry.

A realization that can be as exciting as overwhelming to think about, but which bears huge opportunities to re-align fashion with our true needs and the needs of our planet. What's important is starting in the right direction, which Francesca Romana Rinaldi properly identifies in this book in three key drivers: traceability, circularity and collaborative consumption.

Traceability as the first step to not only give customers the possibility to access verified and truthful information about the supply chain, but also as a tool to map the hidden potential for synergic partnerships which will make circular fashion a reality, in dynamics of symbiotic economy.

Afterword

This book provides the inspiration and the tools for a new generation of leaders in the fashion industry to take on their role with the understanding that they will have to re-imagine it. Opening up the industry to embrace a necessary shift from the current and static situation of linear individualism to a state of circular collectivism, with an inclusive mindset which will see the market, our customers, taking on a more active role – all united in their diversity for a stronger future.

List of Boxes

Chapter 1
Box 1   Sustainable fashion discussed in the scientific literature

Chapter 2
Box 2   Engaging the younger generation in sustainable fashion
Box 3   Main characteristics of consumers interested in sustainability in Italy
Box 4   UN guidelines for providing product sustainability information
Box 5   The interest of young fashion consumers towards sustainability in fashion

Chapter 3
Box 6   Partnership along the pipeline for responsible fashion: Candiani Denim and Dondup D/Zero collaboration
Box 7   Salvatore Ferragamo's commitment towards circular fashion
Box 8   Vestiaire Collective as a best practice for luxury recommerce
Box 9   Responsible innovation at Kering
Box 10   Patagonia's 360° sustainability approach and support to responsible innovation to 'save our home planet'

Chapter 4
Box 11   The ITC Sustainability Map

Chapter 5
Box 12   Martine Jarlgaard and blockchain implementation

Chapter 6

Box 13 The UN and European Commission support of circular economy
Box 14 The principles of eco-design for circularity
Box 15 Patagonia 360° circularity approach
Box 16 Interview with Enrica Arena, co-founder Orange Fiber
Box 17 Interview with Matteo Ward, co-founder and CEO of WRÅD
Box 18 Progetto Quid
Box 19 Stella McCartney: materials and innovation

Chapter 7

Box 20 Accenture's point of view on collaborative consumption
Box 21 Rent the Runway
Box 22 MUD Jeans
Box 23 Eileen Fisher's three lives of a product

Chapter 9

Box 24 Towards the 4th Industrial Revolution: the case of Italy
Box 25 Notes on blockchain, Iot, VR, AI and machine learning technologies

The Authors

Francesca Romana Rinaldi, PhD, is Director of the Master in Fashion Direction: Brand & Business Management and the New Sustainable Fashion short course at Milano Fashion Institute (inter-university consortium among Bocconi University, Cattolica University and Polytechnic of Milan). She teaches at Bocconi University and SDA Bocconi School of Management. She is co-author of *L'Impresa Moda Responsabile* (Egea, 2013) and *The Responsible Fashion Company* (Greenleaf Publishing-Routledge, 2014). She is executive consultant for companies in the Fashion and Luxury industries with a focus on brand management, sustainability, digital strategies and business model innovation.

She is an Expert at the United Nations Economic Commission for Europe (UNECE) on the topic of Responsible Fashion. She is regularly invited as a speaker at international forums and for interviews by Italian TV channels such as RAI, LA7, Canale 5, SKY and some international channels.

In 2010 she has created the Bio-Fashion blog (http://bio-fashion.blogspot.com) with the objective of raising awareness on Sustainability in Fashion and Luxury. In 2019 she has created the Instagram account @fashionindustry_2030 to start a conversation with opinion leaders and experts about the future of fashion.

Matteo Marzotto is Chairman of Dondup since September 2016 and Vice President of Progetto Marzotto Association, which he led from October 2012 to February 2018. After working for fifteen years in various companies owned by the Marzotto family, maturing experiences along the whole textile and clothing supply chain, between 2003 and 2008 he was Chief Operating Officer (COO) and then Chairman of Valentino S.p.A. He is investor in industrial companies and services sectors.

As an entrepreneur, between October 2008 and January 2013 he acquired and re-launched Vionnet S.p.A., of which he was also President. As a civil servant he is among the founders of the Italian Cystic Fibrosis Research Foundation, as well as a permanent Member of the Board of Nuovi Orizzonti-AIPDF (Private International Association of the faithful of pontifical right), and the President of Mittelmoda International Lab. He has served as Councilor and as Chairman of Fondazione CUOA-University Centre of Business Administration, as well as President and Commissioner of the Enit-National Tourism Agency.

He has been honored with numerous awards for his socio-economic activities, including the Academic Seal of the University of Urbino, the Leonardo Italian Quality Award, the Guido Carli Award, the Mother Teresa of Calcutta International Award-Hymn to Life, the Casentino Award. Also, he has been part of the Ambassador team for the World Exposition Expo Milan 2015.

Matteo Ward graduated in International Economics from Bocconi University in 2008 and is today the CEO and co-founder of WRÅD, innovative start-up and design studio dedicated to sustainable innovation and social change, winner of the Best of the Best RedDot Design Award and Green Carpet Challenge Award Finalist. Prior to co-founding WRÅD he pursued a 6-year career with Abercrombie and Fitch where he covered the roles of Senior Manager in Germany and co-chair of the A&F Global Diversity and Inclusion Council. Matteo is a member of Fashion Revolution Italia and Art & Creative Director for the newly launched sustainable hub at the WHITE Milan Trade Show (GIVE A FOKus).

He is often called as a public speaker at international forums, including the United Nations (UNECE framework on traceability), TEDx talk, WIRED Digital Day, Fashion Tech Berlin and Fashion Sustain Berlin.

Maria Teresa Pisani is Acting Head of the Sustainable Trade and Outreach Unit at the Economic Cooperation and Trade Division of UNECE, where she leads the work on policies and standards for sustainable trade facilitation, and is currently managing a global multi-stakeholder initiative on sustainable value chains in the clothing industry. At UNECE since 2011, she has been focusing on trade and environmental governance and worked to the launch of the pan-European green economy strategy.

Before joining the UN, Maria Teresa has been with the European Commission and the ILO, and has managed World Bank funded projects for institutional reforms in developing countries all over the world. Maria Teresa is passionate about art and culture as a means of social transformation and enjoys engaging with young talents.

Iolanda D'Amato is lecturer of Operations and Supply Chain Management and consultant. After graduating in Economics and Business Management from the University of Naples "Federico II", she earned a master's degree in Business Administration from SDA Bocconi and a PhD in Logistics and Supply Chain Management, program run by the University of Bergamo in collaboration with Bocconi University and Massachusetts Institute of Technology – Zaragoza Logistic Centre. Today, she teaches at SDA Bocconi School of Management, Bocconi University and IESEG School of Management.

She has conducted numerous training, research and consulting projects in various fields, including fashion and luxury, media and telecommunications. Her research activities focus on supply chain management, logistics and service operations management. Her many works have been published in International Journal of Retail & Distribution Management, Journal of Business & Industrial Marketing, Economia & Management, Harvard Business Review Italia. Before teaching at SDA Bocconi, she worked as a consultant for large telecommunications companies in Italy, France and Brazil.

Elisabetta Amadei has graduated in Management from Bocconi University in 2018. Deeply passionate about circular economy and its applications, she dedicated her master's thesis and future research works at Bocconi University to this topic. In collaboration with the IEFE research center, she published C.E.R.C.A. Project: Circular Economy as Competitive Resource for Enterprises (2018).

Eric Ezechieli is a regenerative entrepreneur and in 2012, with Paolo Di Cesare, he founded Nativa, the first Certified B Corp and Benefit Corporation in Europe. He has more than twenty years of experience in the field of evolution towards sustainability and leadership development. Chairman of The Natural Step International 2015-2017, G7 Advisor on People Centric Innovation, and Singularity University Faculty Member. After graduating in Business from Bocconi University, he got his master's degree in Innovation for Sustainability at Stanford, California. He is also Alumnus of the Global Solutions Program of Singularity University. Most Valuable Player 2016 of the global B Corp movement for the contribution in the introduction of the new legal status Società Benefit in Italy and The Good Lobby Award 2018 recipient.

P hury

have
a good
day